TRAVELLERS

ROMANIA

D1561359

By
DEBBIE STOWE

Written by Debbie Stowe
Original photography by Vasile Szakacs

Published by Thomas Cook Publishing
A division of Thomas Cook Tour Operations Limited.
Company registration no. 1450464 England
The Thomas Cook Business Park, Unit 9, Coningsby Road,
Peterborough PE3 8SB, United Kingdom
E-mail: books@thomascook.com, Tel: + 44 (0) 1733 416477
www.thomascookpublishing.com

Produced by Cambridge Publishing Management Limited
Burr Elm Court, Main Street, Caldecote CB23 7NU

ISBN: 978-1-84157-931-3

First edition © 2008 Thomas Cook Publishing
Text © Thomas Cook Publishing
Maps © Thomas Cook Publishing/PCGraphics (UK) Limited

Series Editor: Maisie Fitzpatrick
Production/DTP: Steven Collins

Printed and bound in Italy by Printer Trento

Cover photography: Front L–R: © Mehlig Manfred/SIME-4Corners Images,
© Richard I'Anson/Lonely Planet Images, © Mehlig Manfred/SIME-4Corners
Images; Back L–R: © Schmid Reinhard/SIME-4Corners Images, © Mehlig
Manfred/SIME-4Corners Images

The paper used for this book has been independently certified as having
been sourced from well-managed forests and recycled wood or fibre
according to the rules of the Forest Stewardship Council.
This book has been printed and bound in Italy by Printer Trento S.r.l.,
an FSC certified company for printing books on FSC mixed paper in
compliance with the chain of custody and on products labelling standards.

FSC
Mixed Sources
Product group from well-managed
forests and recycled wood or fibre
Cert no. CQ-COC-000012
www.fsc.org
© 1996 Forest Stewardship Council

Contents

Introduction

Few outsiders know much about Romania apart from the usual clichés – Dracula and orphans. Under nearly half a century of Communism, contact between the country and the outside world was strictly limited and monitored. In the chaos since the Romanian Revolution of 1989, when pictures of the dictator Nicolae Ceauşescu waving to the crowds as he slowly realised his regime was crashing down around him were beamed across the world, the country has done little to sell itself abroad.

The upshot of this is that Romania is largely a land undiscovered by tourists. Many people may have heard of the People's Palace – Ceauşescu's behemoth of a vanity project – but few will know about, say, the Athenaeum, the magnificent neo-classical concert hall. Much of the country's beauty is similarly low-key. For all the expected creepy Transylvanian castles, there are spectacular mountain ranges, vividly well-preserved frescoes and international-quality (but Eastern European-priced) restaurants. Not to mention the Danube Delta, Europe's most important wetland, traversed by manifold species of bird. But most of this goes unreported in favour of negative stories about gypsies, monotonous apartment blocks and criminality.

Travelling in Romania is not always easy. Communism left a legacy of poverty, inefficiency and poor service. You may often find yourself baffled by the difficulty of performing seemingly simple, everyday tasks, and it is heartbreaking for a visitor to see the plight of the country's street children.

Old farming traditions survive in Romania

The horse and cart is still a common means of transport in places

But European Union membership, finally achieved in 2007, has given the country new optimism. And it is the people that are likely to be one of the highlights of your trip. Though their directness may initially make them appear brusque, Romanians have a warm Latin spirit that makes them natural and generous hosts. As a guest in their country, the local people will go out of their way to welcome you – and if you end up in a Romanian home, you had better have a big appetite.

This is a country of contradictions and oppositions. While it increasingly embraces the West with its designer labels and conspicuous consumption, there are still wonderfully olde-worlde scenes – the old men's chess club in the park, the family clip-clopping along the road on their horse and cart, rustic cottages outside which the old women sit and gossip. The ugly Communist block stands next to the chic art deco villa. It is this 'anything goes' mentality that makes travelling here so exhilarating, even if it is sometimes a little frustrating.

If you visit Romania now, you will see a country on the cusp of change, as it moves from Communist state to modern democracy. It remains different enough that you will feel that you're experiencing another culture, and yet geographically close enough that it's just a couple of hours by plane from Western Europe. While they're aware of its faults, Romanians are proud of their homeland, if still a little surprised that foreigners come here to visit it. Be relaxed about the irritations and you will discover scenic, cultural and gastronomic delights made all the more special by the warm and welcoming people waiting to show you them.

The land

Romania can be roughly divided into equal portions of mountains, hills, and plains. It is a diverse country, both physically and politically. The flat south, including the capital Bucharest, is dominated by ethnic Romanians. But drive for three hours north and you're suddenly in the middle of mountains, hearing Hungarian spoken. Drive east instead and you're likely to spot a mosque by the beach, catering to a Turkish contingent.

The central area has most of the mountains, which extend northwards to the region that is home to most of the country's famous monasteries. The southeast, including the capital and most important city Bucharest, is low-lying. The east features Romania's only stretch of coastline, the Black Sea coast. The northern part of the shoreline expands eastwards to form the Danube Delta, Europe's main wetland, which is teeming with avian and aquatic life.

Romania has a great deal of picturesque countryside, from dazzling sunflower fields in the southeast to the snow-capped mountains of Transylvania. Rural areas are a hotchpotch of small farms which seem to belong to a bygone age.

Two areas that are comparatively hostile to humans but particularly welcoming to nature underpin Romania's role as an important environment for flora and fauna. The first is the Carpathians. With little incursion from man, significant populations of large carnivores were able to survive and prosper here, even as they were extirpated from much of the rest of Europe. Carpathian deer, brown bears, wolves, hares, black chamois, lynx, boars and foxes all reside in the forest-coated mountain ranges. The second area of note is the Danube Delta, whose ever-changing make-up has provided relief for legions of bird, plant and fish species, including the pelican and caviar-producing sturgeon.

The Danube Delta is home to diverse plant life

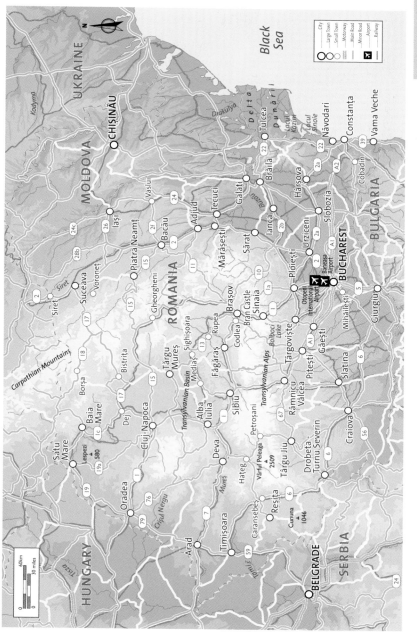

Black Sea

UKRAINE

MOLDOVA

CHIȘINĂU

Kodyma

Drakuliya

D e l t a

D u n ă r i i

Lacul Razim

Lacul Sinoie

Tulcea

Năvodari

Constanța

Vama Veche

Cobadin

BULGARIA

Vaslui

Iași

Bacău

Adjud

Tecuci

Galați

Brăila

Hârșova

Slobozia

Urziceni

Siret

Suceava

Voroneț

Piatra Neamț

Gheorgheni

Mărășești

Sărat

Ianca

Buzău

Ploiești

BUCHAREST

Bănesa Airport

Giurgiu

Mihăilești

ROMANIA

Brașov

Bran Castle

Sinaia

Rupea

Codlea

Bolboci Lake

Târgoviște

Otopeni International Airport

Găești

Câmpina

Borșa

Bistrița

Târgu Mureș

Sighișoara

Mediaș

Făgăraș

Transylvanian Alps

Transylvanian Basin

Râmnicu Vâlcea

Pitești

Slatina

Craiova

Carpathian Mountains

Baia Mare

Dej

Cluj-Napoca

Alba Iulia

Sibiu

Petroșani

Vârful Peleaga 2509

Hațeg

Târgu Jiu

Drobeta-Turnu Severin

Satu Mare

Lespezi 580

Deva

Mureș

Reșița

Caransebeș

Curuna 1046

SERBIA

Oradea

Crișul Negru

Timișoara

Arad

Mureș

BELGRADE

HUNGARY

Tisza

Crișul Alb

City
Large Town
Small Town
Motorway
Main Road
Minor Road
Airport
Railway

60km
30 miles

N

History

Stone Age	The first traces of human habitation in the future Romania.
8000 BC	The country is home to settled communities who make their living from farming and hunting.
3000 BC	The Thracians, a group of Indo-European tribes, travel from Asia and occupy the future Romania.
2000 BC	A Thracian sub-group emerges and becomes known to the Romans as the Dacians, while the Greeks refer to them as the Getae.
700 BC	The Greeks begin to establish trading colonies, particularly along the Black Sea coast. Western-style civilisation begins to develop.
82–44 BC	Burebista rules Dacia, ancient Romania.
AD 100	Dacian civilisation reaches its zenith.
101–106	The Romans invade Dacia.
256	Romans pull out of Dacia as a result of Barbarian invasions.
4th century	The Daco-Roman Latin-speaking people adopt Christianity.
1000	Three distinct principalities, Moldavia, Wallachia, and Transylvania, emerge, the latter being under Hungarian and German control.
12th century	Saxon settlers from Germany start to establish towns in Transylvania, at the behest of the King of Hungary.
1448, 1456–62, 1476	The three reigns of Vlad Ţepeş (Vlad the Impaler), the Wallachian ruler who would subsequently inspire the Dracula myth.
1457–1504	Reign of Moldavian Prince Ştefan cel Mare (Stephen the Great). He builds monasteries to commemorate his many victories on the battlefield.
1600	The three principalities are united for the first time, for six months, by Mihai

	Viteazul (Michael the Brave).
17th century	Having triumphed over the Ottomans, the Austrian Habsburgs try to increase their own empire, and seize Transylvania.
1718	The Habsburgs occupy Oltenia, in Wallachia, for almost 20 years.
1775	The Habsburgs gain control of Bucovina.
1812	Basarabia, in Moldavia, is seized by the Russians.
1848	The country is engulfed in the wave of European revolutions stirring liberal, nationalist and socialist movements. In Romania, a bourgeoning bourgeoisie calls for a united country. Transylvania comes under the direct rule of Hungary.
1859	Moldavia and Wallachia unite, led by Prince Alexandru Ioan Cuza.
1866	Cuza abdicates, and is succeeded by a German of the Hohenzollern-Sigmaringen house, Prince Carol I.
1877–8	Romania fights with Russia against the Turks.
1878	The Treaty of Berlin recognises the complete independence of the principalities of Romania.
1881	The country becomes a kingdom, with Carol I on the throne.
1914	King Carol I dies, and is succeeded by his nephew King Ferdinand I.
1916	Romania enters World War I, fighting on the side of the Allies.
1918	Romania is forced to negotiate peace with Germany, before subsequently rejoining the war. The close of hostilities sees Romania awarded territory that doubles its size and population.
Interwar period	*România Mare*, a period of cultural, political and architectural advancement for the country. However, tension surrounding the ethnic minorities is increasing, and with it comes the growth of Fascism.

1930	Carol II succeeds his father, Ferdinand, as king.
1938	Under pressure from the rise of Fascism, King Carol II abolishes parliament and declares a dictatorship.
1940	Romania cedes territories to both Hungary and the USSR. Military General Ion Antonescu forces the king to step down in favour of his son, Prince Mihai. Antonescu, however, assumes power himself.
1941	Aiming to retrieve the area lost to the USSR, Romania joins World War II on the side of the Germans.
1944	Having won the backing of pro-Allied politicians including the Communists, King Mihai has Antonescu arrested. Romania switches sides to join the Allies.
1945	At the end of the war, the leaders of the victorious nations, Franklin D Roosevelt, Winston Churchill and Joseph Stalin, meet at the Yalta Conference. Their division of post-war Europe hands Romania to the Russians.
1947	Romania gets Transylvania back from Hungary. After a gradual seizing of power, the Communists force King Mihai to abdicate. They proclaim a Communist People's Republic.
1953	Joseph Stalin dies. Romania starts to distance itself from Moscow.
1965	The prime minister and Communist Party leader Gheorghe Gheorghiu-Dej dies, to be succeeded by Nicolae Ceauşescu.
1966	The spelling of the country's name is officially changed from Rumania to Romania.
1971	Following a tour of China, North Korea and Vietnam, Ceauşescu adopts a more stringent brand of Communism. He instils a personality cult and starts to have large areas demolished in a process of systematisation.
1977	Bucharest is rocked by an earthquake which kills around 1,500 people.

1980s Ceauşescu's determination to pay off the national debt and enthusiasm for vanity projects sees a huge amount of Romanian goods exported, leaving the country in severe deprivation. The regime becomes more oppressive.

1989 The Romanian Revolution sees a week of rebellion and riots that culminate in the show trial and execution of Nicolae and Elena Ceauşescu.

1990 Former Communist official Ion Iliescu seizes power. He summons the country's miners to violently suppress academics who protest against ex-Communists returning to office.

1991 Low salaries and the high cost of living prompt miners' riots. The government collapses.

1992 Iliescu voted in for another term.

1996 Centre-right Romanian Democratic Convention (CDR) beats the ex-Communists (PSD) in the general election.

1997 The CDR initiates major reforms and opens Securitate (Communist Secret Police) files.

1999 The European Union invites Romania to begin negotiations on the country's accession.

2000 Iliescu is re-elected, beating the other presidential finalist, far-right candidate Corneliu Vadim Tudor.

2002 Romania receives official invitation to join NATO.

2004 Romania joins NATO. PSD loses general election to Justice and Truth Alliance. Iliescu is replaced as president by Traian Băsescu, mayor of Bucharest.

2007 Romania accedes to the EU. Parliament suspends Băsescu, on charges of violating the constitution. He wins the vote returning him to office. After a postponement due to political upheaval at home, Romania holds its first ever elections for the European Parliament.

Politics

Romanian politics has always been about personalities rather than policies and expedient coalitions have been formed between the least likely of political bedfellows. Corruption is never far from the surface and various high-ranking political figures have been accused of influence-peddling in business dealings, suppressing the media, vote-rigging, links with the Securitate (Communist Secret Police) and other wrong-doing.

The country's current political formation began to take shape in 1990, after the Romanian Revolution had overthrown the Communist regime and executed its leader Nicolae Ceauşescu and his wife Elena. Much about the revolution (including suspicions of involvement from foreign parties and the identity of mysterious gunmen) remains unclear to this day. What is clear is that just days after the Ceauşescus were ousted, former Communists led by Ion Iliescu had seized power by gaining control of the only TV channel on air at the time and making pronouncements. Iliescu's newly established group, the National Salvation Front, was supposed to organise general elections in 1990 and stand down. However, it ended up contesting and – with the help of a media monopoly – winning them.

The former Communists continued to dominate the local political landscape. When students and professors protested at how the revolution was being hijacked, Iliescu called the miners to Bucharest to suppress the demonstrating 'hooligans', which they violently did. Iliescu's party again triumphed at the 1992 elections, before being voted out four years later,

The Romanian flag adorns many public buildings

The Government building in Bucharest, which houses the Cabinet

owing in large part to the beginnings of an independent media. New President Emil Constantinescu began a far-reaching reform programme. However, the coalition government was beset by in-fighting, living standards continued to fall and political disenchantment fomented. In the 2000 elections the ex-Communist PSD won and Iliescu returned for another four years.

In 2004, following Romania's acceptance into NATO, the PSD lost to the Justice and Truth Alliance headed by Traian Băsescu who became president. But the squabbling continued, as the alliance collapsed and disparate parties colluded to suspend Băsescu. One of the few politicians to be genuinely popular with the voters, Băsescu easily won the public vote to overturn the suspension and returned to office. However, his tenure continues to be dominated by in-fighting, particularly his feud with Prime Minister Călin Popescu-Tăriceanu,

whom Băsescu appointed but does not have the right to dismiss.

The system in place is a parliamentary representative democratic republic. The president safeguards the observance of the Constitution and the proper functioning of the public authorities. He acts as a mediator between the state powers, as well as the state and the public. The prime minister leads the government, which exercises executive power. Legislative power is shared between the government and parliament, which is comprised of the Chamber of Deputies and the Senate. The judiciary is theoretically separate from both the executive and the legislature, although there have been accusations of interference. Voting takes place every four years for general elections, every five for presidential ones. Proportional representation is the system used, something that four out of five Romanians would like to see changed, according to a 2007 poll.

Culture

Culture in Romania is still trying to recover from the oppression of Communism. However, the country had a thriving cultural life in the interwar period, when foreign architects were responsible for a plethora of beautiful buildings and middle-class urbanites debated French literature. Some of this spirit lives on today, holding its own against the huge enthusiasm for American and Western offerings.

Arts and crafts

While the country has a few world-renowned artists, particularly Constantin Brâncuşi, one of the spearheads of modern sculpture (*see pp94–5*), the essence of Romanian life is summed up best by its arts and crafts, which are still going strong in some of the remoter, rural areas. Pottery and ceramics are mostly made using traditional kickwheels, and finished off with simple tools. Designs vary by the area in which they are produced, but often include floral patterns and simple human and animal figures. Apart from the ubiquitous presence of iconography, the tradition of painted eggs (hollowed out, rather than the hard-boiled variety eaten by families at Easter) underlines the strong influence religion has on the country's art and culture. Again, the intricate patterns have regional variations.

Woodwork, the main origins of which are in the timber-rich northern region of Maramureş, is used not only in a purely decorative capacity, but is integrated into the household, in kitchen utensils and furniture. The showpiece item was historically the gate, the level of its elaborateness conveying the family's status in the community. The symbols used in items of woodcraft encapsulate the country's respect for superstition; moons, wolves' teeth, flowers and stars were among the motifs used for luck or to ward off evil. Masks, usually hewn from animal hide, play a similar symbolic role in festivals, particularly in Maramureş and Moldavia.

Theatre

Despite its late advent, Romanian theatre developed quickly. The first proper performances came in the 1810s. The encouraging cultural climate of the time saw the emergence of top playwrights and actors and frequent visits from foreign troupes. Under Communism, many of the big names in drama left the country. Eugen

Ionescu, one of the foremost writers in the Theatre of the Absurd, was one of the exiles, dividing his time between Romania and France, where he 'francofied' his name to Eugène Ionesco. There are now said to be over 50 theatres around the country, including some spearheaded by ethnic minorities. A few foreign-language productions are also staged.

Cinema

Local films have made a big splash internationally in recent years. Cristian Mungiu's *4 luni, 3 săptămâni şi 2 zile* (*4 Months, 3 Weeks and 2 Days*) won the Palme d'Or at Cannes in 2007, following on from the success of *Moartea domnului Lăzărescu* (*The Death of Mr Lazarescu*) at the same festival two years before. The local film industry is explored in more depth on pp44–5.

Architecture

The mishmash of ethnic influences Romania has undergone has left its mark on the buildings, from the Saxon houses of Transylvania to the Byzantine touches in the south, and from the shiny tin roofs of Roma homes to the foreign-inspired art deco buildings of Bucharest. But what makes the greatest visual impact are the legions of demoralisingly monotonous grey Communist blocks that dominate the skyline of most cities. High-ranking Communists of course did not live in such dreary places. The élite were housed in superior blocks, some of which make up the Communist centre of Bucharest, a Ceauşescu vanity project that had the main boulevard deliberately built a metre wider than the Champs-Élysées. At the end of it stands the People's Palace, called by one guidebook 'the world's largest eyesore'. Wandering around this area gives a revealing insight into the psyche of the former regime. The disparity of income is also clear in Romania's architecture, which runs the gamut from hovels, with no running water or electricity, to gaudy mansions for the nouveau riche.

A Transylvanian potter at work in his studio

Culture

Literature

Modern Romanian literature, which began when Latin replaced Cyrillic as the official Romanian alphabet in 1860, was initially influenced both by peasant traditions and French writing.

The two main luminaries were 19th-century writers Mihai Eminescu and Ion Luca Caragiale, both of whom have a surfeit of streets named after them. Eminescu was a late-Romantic poet, whose themes were nature, love, history, social commentary and nostalgia. Schoolchildren today have to learn his poems off by heart, and he also features on the 500 lei banknote (the highest-value bill). Caragiale, who wrote plays and short stories, was ironic and provocative. His output displeased the establishment and he eventually left Romania for Berlin. Much of modern Romanian literature is concerned with the effects of Communism.

A mandolin player helps keep Romania's musical traditions alive

Music

Early folk music featured different pipes, with rhythmical accompaniment from a lute. Flutes and especially violins are now the most common folk instruments. Traditional music varies significantly from region to region. Themes include love and drinking. Simple, communal dances are often performed, which may involve participants forming a circle or line, arms draped around each other's shoulders. It is not easy to come across a live performance, unless you are invited to a traditional Romanian wedding, but 24-hour cable channel Etno TV, accessible in many hotels and homes, will give you a glimpse.

Classical music also has a strong tradition, not least because of the links between Transylvania and Austria and Germany, with Sibiu in particular a centre and stop-off point for top composers and musicians. Among local-born practitioners, composer, violinist, pianist and conductor George Enescu is widely considered one of the greatest performers of his time. Inspired by local folk music, he studied in Paris, composing highly esteemed rhapsodies and an opera among his canon. Enescu is celebrated once every two years in an eponymous classical music festival.

Modern music is heavily influenced by Western sounds. After years of censorship, rock and hip-hop galvanised the frustrated youth and both foreign bands and local versions

Constantin Brâncuși's striking *Infinite Column* in Târgu Jiue

have huge and enthusiastic followings. Most urban radio stations play predominantly English-language pop and occasional derivative Romanian versions, although rural stations play more local music. The other strain of contemporary music is more Eastern in flavour; *manele*, primarily a Roma genre, is descended from Turkish and Arab love songs. Themes are usually limited to desirable women (the singers are mostly male) and self-aggrandisement. *Manele*'s misogyny, kitsch style and bad grammar infuriate many intellectuals, but the genre remains hugely popular among the Roma and lower-class Romanians. For that reason, it has been compared with rock-and-roll and particularly rap.

Festivals and events

For the most eye-catching festivals, you really have to head for the countryside, where bizarre traditions and rituals have survived modernisation. Religious occasions are taken particularly seriously, and Romanians celebrate the saints' days (after whom many are named) as a birthday. As well as rural revelry, there are some up-to-the-minute cultural events, showcasing drama, film, music and jazz.

January
Winter Sports Festival: Câmpulung Moldovenesc, last Sunday.

February
Enchanted Water Springs Music Festival: Târgu Jiu, third Sunday.

March
Mărțișor: heralds the beginning of spring. Men present any women they meet with a gift, usually a small flower with a red and white string, also called a *mărțișor*. 1 March.
International Women's Day: sees men again giving flowers to all the women with whom they interact. 8 March.

March–May
As in other Orthodox countries, **Easter** is a bigger deal than Christmas in Romania. Families paint the shells of hard-boiled eggs, which they then crack against each other in a game, the winner being the one whose egg withstands the impact. The eggs are then eaten. There's a night-long service on Saturday, and many restaurants close for the period, as families stay home and eat lamb and eggs – lots of them.

April
Rooster Shooting: near Brașov, third Sunday.
St George's Day: Sfântu Gheorghe, last Sunday.

April–May
A tradition dating back hundreds of years, **Sărbătoarea Junilor** (Pageant of the Juni) sees the bachelors of Brașov parade in flamboyant armour and on horseback through the city.

May
Constanța Days: around 21 May.
Gayfest: Bucharest, late May/early June.
Sibiu Jazz Festival: varies.

June

Romania's only international feature film festival, **Transylvania International Film Festival** in Sibiu aims to promote young filmmakers and showcase innovative, original and independent new features.

Suceava Days: music, dance and craft fair, late June.

July

Maramuzical Festival: Maramureş, mid-July.

Medieval Festival of the Arts: Sighişoara, late July.

August

Liberty Parade: Vame Veche, late July/early August.

Sfântu Gheorghe Film Festival: Danube Delta, varies.

September

The **George Enescu International Festival**: named after Romania's most famous composer, is held biennially, for two or three weeks at the beginning of September in Bucharest. Orchestras and performers from across Europe play and compete in daily concerts.

Sâmbra Oilor (Welcoming of the Sheep): Tara Oaşului, late September/early October.

October/November

National Theatre Festival: Bucharest.

December

Moş Nicolae (St Nicholas's Day) On 6 December parents fill their children's polished boots with small gifts, and a stick to warn the recipient to behave well throughout the year. On Christmas Eve people go to church and decorate their trees.

Winter Festival: Maramureş, 27 December.

Dancers in traditional costumes at the Maramuzical Festival

Highlights

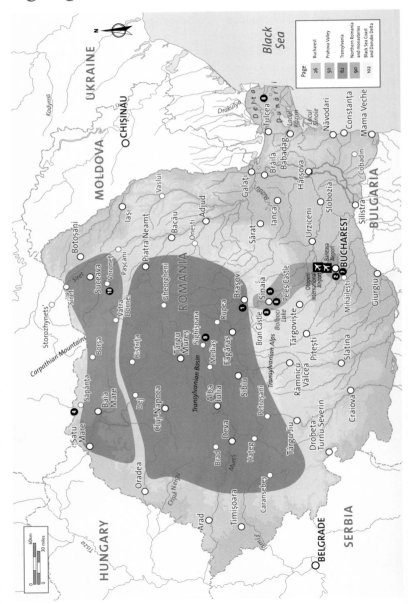

❶ Braşov town centre
A million miles from the traffic-clogged capital, a stroll through the old town of Braşov recalls a peaceful, sleepier Romania. Take a day or two and unwind after the frenetic capital (*see pp64–8*).

❷ Bucharest art deco
Though more infamous for its ugly blocks and the enormous People's Palace, Bucharest is teeming with beautiful, interwar buildings of style and grace. A meander round the back streets of the city centre will yield architectural delights (*see pp26–47*).

❸ Castelul Bran (Bran Castle)
The somewhat tenuous connection to Dracula does not take away from the fact that this castle ticks all the right creepy, vampiric boxes. Witty guides happily ham up the myth (*see pp68–9*).

❹ Cimitirul Vesel (Merry Cemetery)
The dazzling and pretty gravestones at the Merry Cemetery in Săpânţa celebrate life rather than mourn death. To get the most out of it, go with a Romanian speaker who can translate the irreverent inscriptions (*see p92*).

❺ Cota 1400, Sinaia
Wolves, bears and the Dracula myth combine to add a hint of mystery and menace to the stunning mountain views that continuously surprise and delight visitors and locals alike. Enjoy the sights on a leisurely drive up to Cota 1400, then enjoy a leisurely lunch looking out over the panorama (*see pp56–7*).

❻ Danube Delta bird-watching
With over 300 species of birds frequenting the area, the Danube Delta is equally beguiling for expert ornithologists or laymen who enjoy the idea of tranquillity, birdsong and messing about in boats. European waterways don't get much richer than this (*see pp107–9*).

❼ Casa Poporului (People's Palace)
It has been described as a giant eyesore and a monument to madness, but the colossal People's Palace, Europe's largest building, is still an awe-inspiring sight. For an insight into the mind of a megalomaniac, take the fascinating tour (*see pp31–2*).

❽ Palatul Peleş (Peleş Castle)
Previously an elegant home for Romania's royals, the beautiful Peleş Castle and its 160 rooms, some of which can be explored, easily hold their own against any West European counterparts.

The tour offers a melange of olden-day interior design (*see pp55–6*).

❾ Sighişoara medieval citadel
An imposing clock tower, Saxon fortifications and the birthplace of Vlad Ţepeş (Vlad the Impaler) are a few of the draws of this well-preserved and atmospheric medieval town, a UNESCO World Heritage Site (*see pp83–7*).

❿ Voroneţ
Gothic spires, vivid frescoes and an excellent state of preservation characterise the churches of Romania's north, of which Voroneţ is arguably the best. Here the way of life seems as little changed as the churches (*see p99*).

The Orthodox church of Sighişoara

Suggested itineraries

Long weekend

Owing to Romania's relatively large size and the poor condition of some of its roads, it is not the easiest country in which to nip about. What's more, many of its highlights are off the beaten track. But even if your time is limited, provided you structure it well, you can have a rewarding mini-break and still experience, in small doses, a lot of what the country has to offer. For those on a more relaxed schedule, the little-known delights of Romania will prove more than rewarding.

If you have only a weekend or so in Romania it is likely that your starting point will be Bucharest. Although it is much maligned, there is plenty to see and do in this lesser-known European capital, and it is certainly worth spending a day or two here. The must-see is the Casa Poporului, Ceauşescu's gargantuan vanity project. If you have time, take the 45-minute tour of the interior.

Provided the weather is bearable, your next stop should be the outdoor Village Museum. Not only does it make for an enjoyable couple of hours in its own right, but the collection of 60-plus original homes, farms, churches and other buildings from across the country presents a microcosm of rural Romanian architecture. If the 15 ha (37 acres) of museum tire you out, take a break in one of the boutique cafés in the Lipscani district, Bucharest's historical heart. The area also merits a stroll for its cobbled alleys, antique-cum-junk shops full of curios, and shabby-chic houses. Depending on your interests, you may also want to take in the Muzeului Naţional de Artă al Românei (National Art Gallery), Muzeul Ţăranului Romăn (Peasant Museum) or Grădina Cişmigiu (Cişmigiu Gardens).

For dinner, the twice-weekly Dracula Show at Count Dracula Club (*see p149*) is hilariously kitsch. Alternatively, Caru' Cu Bere (*see p159*) offers traditional Romanian food in a fabulous historic building. But if the local fare doesn't appeal, there are at

Thousands of Romanians flock to the Black Sea coast every summer

The Casa Poporului is the country's most famous (or infamous) landmark

least a dozen top-class international restaurants from which to choose. After your meal – and if you have the energy – head to a basement dive bar or, if it's summer, enjoy a few drinks on a terrace.

If your stay is short, it's better to take taxis from place to place rather than try to fathom the sometimes complicated public transport system. Some of the central places can be visited on foot.

Unless you have just two days in the country, you will probably want to see something other than the capital. The best choice on a long weekend is Braşov, around two hours from Bucharest by train or car. There is plenty to see around the city centre, which is small enough to explore on foot. You don't want to leave Braşov without seeing Bran Castle, about an hour's drive away from the city. En route you'll pass the fortress at Râşnov, the climb to which is fairly tiring. Buses go between Braşov and Bran,

but if you're in a group, it may be worth negotiating with a taxi driver to take you there and back.

One week

With a week you can also fit in one other destination, perhaps two if you have your own transport and don't mind rushing. If it's summer, you could pay a visit to the seaside. Hippies and other admirers of counterculture should go for Vama Veche, a sort of Eastern European Goa, replete with dreadlocks, DJs and nude bathing (although technically prohibited). If you enjoy decent food and a wider choice of activities, head for Mamaia. In spring or autumn, a better choice would be the Danube Delta, as these are peak avian seasons. In winter, break your journey to Braşov at Sinaia. Not only does it have two great castles and a monastery, but you can also go skiing. While things are easier with your own car, this trip is easily done on trains, buses and maxi-taxis.

Two weeks

Extend your stays in Bucharest and Braşov, and see some of the smaller, more esoteric museums. Depending on the season, you can visit the coast, another mountain resort and even the Danube. You'll be able to reach remoter – and often more rewarding – parts of the country, particularly with your own transport. If you choose to do so, it is worth considering a homestay. Some such places are in tiny villages, and afford an authentic glimpse of real Romania. You can also extend your Transylvania foray further. Sibiu and Sighişoara are both beautiful medieval towns; if you have to pick one go for Sibiu, as it has a livelier cultural scene. In two weeks you can also plan to take in a festival (*see pp18–19*).

Longer

A longer trip of, say, a month, gives you the chance to get all around the country. On top of all the aforementioned locations, you can go further west to Cluj, Timişoara and Oradea. You can also head north and see the striking monasteries for which the country is famous, in Maramureş and Bucovina. There are places, and the north is one of them, where having a car will make things much easier, but a month gives you time to do the trip using public transport. You could even take a train or two – woefully time-consuming but a wonderful way to see a colourful slice of Romanian life and some tiny hamlets. You can plan your route to see any festivals that take your fancy as well.

By simply wandering in the suburbs, you'll get a much truer picture of Romanian life than if you stick to the tourist trail. Of course there are some areas in which it might be unwise to wander; check with your hotel before you set off.

The Transylvanian town of Braşov is always high on visitors' must-see lists

Bucharest

Bucharest may be traffic-clogged, hectic and blighted by ugly Communist blocks, but its many little-known attractions make it worth putting up with the irritations. The Old Town boasts cobbled streets and beautiful art deco and neo-classical gems that once earned the city the moniker 'the Paris of the East'. Bucharest's ever-more sophisticated cultural and culinary scenes are further reasons to spend time in the Romanian capital.

As well as the museums, cafés, restaurants and shopping of a European capital, the city also has various picturesque streets through which to wander and pleasant green spaces in which to rest a while. The thoughtless nature of the town planning – a stunning art deco villa could be set off by a hideous 1970s monstrosity right next to it – gives the town an eclectic charm. Bucharest has the 24-hour atmosphere of a modern metropolis; you can get a beer or loaf of bread at any time of the day or night, and the latest technology is eagerly embraced. But it also looks back to a bygone age, in the crumbling architecture and old men's chess club in the park.

Orientation

Despite a relatively large population of around two million, Bucharest is a compact city, and many of its main attractions are within walking distance of each other. A central axis runs north to south through the city's four main squares – Piaţa Victoriei to Romana to Universităţii to Unirii – a useful and simple layout for visitors trying to get their bearings. If you get lost, try to spot the Hotel Intercontinental, the city's tallest building, which marks Piaţa Universităţii. Another unmistakable sight is the People's Palace, a huge monolith visible from much of the capital.

The Arcul de Triumf illustrates Romania's French leanings

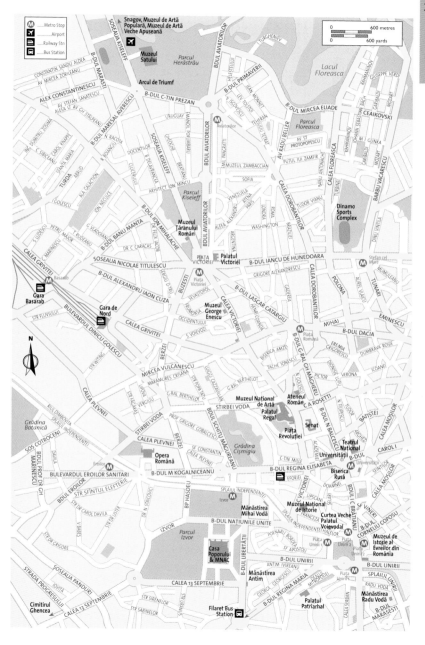

Metro Stop
Airport
Railway Stn
Bus Station

0 ___ 600 metres
0 ___ 600 yards

Snagov, Muzeul de Artă
Populară, Muzeul de Artă
Veche Apuseană

Muzeul
Satului

Parcul
Herăstrău

Lacul
Floreasca

Arcul de Triumf

B-DUL C-TIN PREZAN

SOSEAUA KISELEFF

B-DUL MARASTI

CONSTANTIN SANDU ALDEA

AV MIRCEA ZORILEANU

ALEX CONSTANTINESCU

AV STEFAN SANATESCU

ALEEA 13 AV GH STILPEANU

BDUL AVIATORILOR

B-DUL PRIMAVERII

JEAN MONNET

LEV TOLSTOI

B-DUL MIRCEA ELIADE

CEAIKOVSKI

GIUSEPPE VERDI

Parcul
Floreasca

B-DUL ION MIHALACHE

SOSEAUA KISELEFF

Parcul
Kiseleff

MUZEUL ZAMBACCIAN

SOFIA

MUZEUL
Țăranului
Român

BDUL AVIATORILOR

WASHINGTON

Dinamo
Sports
Complex

CALEA FLOREASCA

CALEA DOROBANTILOR

SOSEAUA NICOLAE TITULESCU

PIATA
VICTORIEI

Palatul
Victoriei

B-DUL IANCU DE HUNEDOARA

Ștefan cel
Mare

B-DUL ALEXANDRU IAON CUZA

Piata
Victoriei

GRIGORE ALEXANDRESCU

CALEA DOROBANTILOR

POLONA

CALEA GRIVITEI

Basarab

Gara
Basarab

BULEVARDUL DINICU GOLESCU

Gara de
Nord

CALEA GRIVITEI

B-DUL LASCAR CATARGIU

Muzeul
George
Enescu

CALEA VICTORIEI

Piata
Romana

B-DUL DACIA

EMINESCU

B-DUL G.RAL GH MAGHERU

MIRCEA VULCANESCU

Grădina
Botanică

CALEA PLEVNEI

STIRBEI VODA

Muzeul National
de Artă

Ateneul
Român

Palatul
Regal

Piata
Revolutiei

Senat

Teatrul
National

Universității

CAROL I

CALEA MOSILOR

Eroilor

Opera
Română

B-DUL M KOGALNICEANU

Grădina
Cișmigiu

C-TIN MILLE

B-DUL REGINA ELISABETA

Universitatii

B-DUL

Biserica
Rusă

BULEVARDUL EROILOR SANITARI

Grădina
Botanică

SOS COTROCENI

BDUL PROF DR CH MARINESCU

BDUL EROILOR

SPLAIUL INDEPENDENTEI

Izvor

Mănăstirea
Mihai Vodă

B-DUL NATIUNILE UNITE

Muzeul National
de Istorie

Curtea Veche
Palatul
Voievodal

B-DUL C BRATIANU

Muzeul de
Istorie al
Evreilor din
România

Parcul
Izvor

Casa
Poporului
& MNAC

B-DUL LIBERTATII

Piata
Unirii 1

Piata
Unirii 2

B-DUL UNIRII

SPLAIUL UNIRII

CALEA 13 SEPTEMBRIE

Mănăstirea
Antim

B-DUL REGINA MARIA

Palatul
Patriarhal

Mănăstirea
Radu Vodă

B-DUL MARASESTI

Cimitirul
Ghencea

SOSEAUA PANDURI

CALEA 13 SEPTEMBRIE

Filaret Bus
Station

N

Walk: historical Bucharest

The comparatively small centre of Bucharest is incredibly diverse, with the Old Town a startling juxtaposition to the vast and orderly Communist civic centre.

Allow about half a day, a full day if you stop and go inside the attractions.

Start at the front entrance of the Hilton (Metro: Piaţa Română. Bus: 122, 178, 300).

1 Ateneul Român

The neo-classical concert hall and pleasant gardens will feature among your best holiday snaps (*see p30*).
Walk down Calea Victoriei. Piaţa Revoluţiei is on your left.

2 Piaţa Revoluţiei

Famous as the square where the people finally turned on Ceauşescu (*see p42*). To the east you'll see the balcony from which he gave his last speech. The west of the square contains the Royal Palace, housing the National Art Museum (*see p37*). The sculpture in the middle is *Memorialul Renaşterii*, the *Rebirth Memorial* (*see p41*).
Keep walking down Calea Victoriei. At the intersection with Regina Elisabeta, turn left and walk until you reach Piaţa Universităţii.

3 Piaţa Universităţii

The university is on your left and you will see the National Theatre in front. A black cross commemorating the first victim of the revolution stands further up the street past the hotel and theatre.
Turn right down Bulevardul Brătianu. The fifth road on your right is Strada Lipscani.

4 Lipscani

Cobbled Lipscani's small alleys and junk shops are wonderfully vibrant. Hanul Şerban Voda, which houses the National Bank of Romania (*No 25*), is a neo-classical joy with imposing Corinthian columns. If you're flagging, stop for a break in one of the boutique cafés.
Turn left onto Strada Smardan and immediately right.

5 Biserica Stavropoleos

Built in Brâncovenesc style, this 18th-century church is home to wall paintings salvaged from the churches the Communists destroyed.
Continue to the main road and turn left. Turn left again along Splaiul Independenţei Halelor, then right into Bulevardul Cantemir, then right again.

6 Piața Unirii

The heart of Ceaușescu's civic centre is a vast square, containing a park, pools and fountains, designed to showcase the 'Victory of Socialism', the name of the street leading east. A short walk from the square's southwest corner is the prepossessing Patriarchal Cathedral.

Take the street running east to the People's Palace.

7 Casa Poporului

It may be tasteless but the sheer proportions of this monument to megalomania are awe-inspiring (*see pp31–2*).

Follow Libertății to the river, then cross the river and turn right into Regina Elisabeta.

8 Grădina Cișmigiu

Relax with a drink on a terrace or on a pedalo in the city's prettiest park.

Leaving the park by the northern entrance, turn right to return to the Hilton.

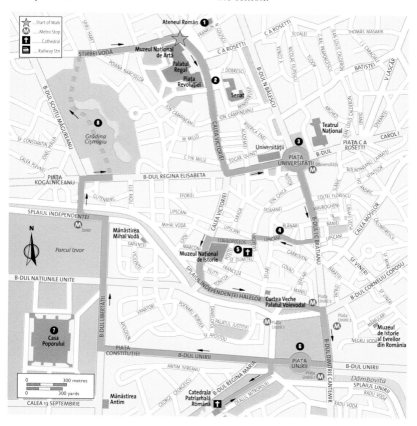

NADIA COMĂNECI

While little distracts Romanians from football, the exploits of one girl have given them a hero from a very different discipline. Nadia Comăneci became famous around the globe as the first gymnast to be awarded a perfect ten in an Olympic gymnastic event, and to this day remains one of the world's most famous gymnasts. She took up the sport at six and was in training at seven, soon taking part in competitions and meets in the region, and later around the world. Her zenith came in the 1976 Montreal Olympics. The scoreboards were not built to display the figure ten, and her record-breaking seven perfect scores were expressed as ones. She was just 14.

Ateneul Român (Athenaeum)

It is best visited in the context of going to hear one of the regular classical music concerts, but the majestic Athenaeum can also be viewed solely as a tourist destination. Designed by a French architect, it is predominantly neo-classical but also has romantic and neo-baroque elements, including a stunning cupola. Don't forget to look up or you'll miss the series of 25 frescoes that depicts various episodes from Romanian history. The statue in front of the entrance is of the national poet, Mihai Eminescu. The grace and sophistication of the Athenaeum is a striking counterpoint to the People's Palace, with which Bucharest is predominantly associated. If either building has a claim to belong to the people, it is the Athenaeum, which was completed with public donations after the funds of the original sponsors were exhausted.
Strada Benjamin Franklin 1–3. Tel: (021) 315 8798. Open: 10am–6pm. Admission charge. Metro: Piaţa Romană.

Ateneul Român is held by many to be Bucharest's most beautiful building

Biserica Rusă (Russian Church)

Bucharest is brimming with beautiful churches that are worthy of a visit, but the Russian Church, also known as St Nicolas Students' Church, stands out on aesthetic grounds. The seven shiny onion domes, typical of the Russian style, probably make the church the most distinctive in the city. The wooden iconostasis is covered in gold, in a style said to be based on the Church of the Twelve Apostles in the Kremlin. The church is open to visitors, and you may even catch a service.

Strada Ion Ghica 9. Open: 9 or 9.30am–8pm, festival days 8am–10pm, services Wed & Fri 7am, Sat & Sun 8am, Tue–Sat 6pm or 7pm, Easter, Christmas Day & Saints' days 8pm. Metro: Universităţii.

The distinctive domes of the Biserica Rusă

Bulevardul Magheru

The main shopping street for the average Bucharestian (Calea Victoriei, which runs parallel, is home to mainly designer shops, far out of the reach of most local pockets), Bulevardul Magheru is busy 24 hours a day. Its shops are a mixture, ranging from austere Communist-style department stores to cheap and cheerful clothes shops selling the latest imports, and global staples such as The Body Shop and Nike. The shoppers are similarly diverse, and strolling up and down (or even sitting – there are a few benches) affords a fair overview of the capital's citizens.

Highlights include the church of St Gheorghe, about halfway down the street on the east side, and the bookshop Cărtureşti (set back from the street near the Patria Cinema), with its café offering an excellent and very international selection of teas. In December, cheery Christmas lights are hung across the boulevard. Somewhat surprisingly, given the street's lack of exclusivity, it was ranked in a survey as the 30th most expensive street in the world on which to rent commercial space.

Metro: Piaţa Romană, Universităţii.

Casa Poporului (People's Palace)

Bucharest's most (some would say only) famous building is notorious as the enormous vanity project that

The grave of Nicolae Ceauşescu

formed the centrepiece of Ceauşescu's envisaged civic centre. Work started on it in 1984, and at the time of the dictator's execution it was about half finished. When Communism fell, the authorities were not sure what to do with the building, but as it was calculated that it would cost as much to demolish it as to finish it, construction continued. Today it is still not entirely finished.

Some of the trivia surrounding the monolith affords a frightening insight into the megalomania of its conceiver. One staircase was ripped out and replaced three times because the Ceauşescus were not happy with the height of the steps, and the central room on the ground floor was designed to have an echo so that ten people clapping would generate the sound of a hundred. Only Romanian materials were used in the building and furnishing and it is said that so much marble was sucked into the project that during the early construction period tombstones had to be made of something else. There are also entirely incongruous religious frescoes on the wall; these are in fact props, put up by a film crew who used the palace as a set for the picture *Amen*, and were never taken down.

Despite the building's almost universally agreed ugliness (writers have remarked on the 'combination of cultural and aesthetic illiteracy, rigid Marxist-Leninist orthodoxy and an innate taste for gigantism' and the 'staggeringly totalitarian frump of an exterior'), it is certainly worth taking the 45-minute tour. (Be warned that there is a lot of climbing involved.) Unless there is an event on, you will be able to go onto the balcony, which offers a fantastic view of the city, and from where Michael Jackson is apocryphally said to have greeted fans with 'Hello Budapest!' (in fact he made the gaffe at the national stadium). As well as housing parliament, rooms in the palace are now let out for various events. (Capitalist giant Coca-Cola launched a product here, which surely would have had Ceauşescu turning in his grave.) Tours in English depart every hour or so.
Calea 13 Septembrie 1. Tel: (021) 311 3611. Open: 10am–4pm. Admission charge. Metro: Izvor. Bus: 385.

Cimitirul Ghencea
(Ghencea Cemetery)

The cemetery's chief draw is that it is the final resting place of Nicolae and Elena Ceaușescu, as well as their son Nicu. Pass through the main entrance, walk forward towards the chapel, and the dictator's grave is on the left-hand side, in row I-35, demarcated by two black crosses and a small black fence. The old matriarchs who sit around the cemetery will point you in the right direction (in the hope of a small tip) if you can't find it. It is still lovingly tended by devotees, who lay flowers and light candles. The same cannot be said for the burial place of Elena, across the other side of the main walkway. The cemetery also has a military wing, where the resting places of former airmen are marked not with headstones but with bright propeller blades.

Calea 13 Septembrie. Tel: (021) 413 8590. Open: 8am–8pm. Free admission. Bus: 385, 173.

Grădina Botanică
(Botanical Gardens)

The gardens' rather turbulent history (uprooted from their former location in 1884, damaged by the Germans in World War I and bombed by the Allies in World War II) is scarcely visible today. Now in the Cotroceni district, home to the president, who lives close by in Cotroceni Palace, they are a

(*Continued p36*)

Families come to Grădina Cișmigiu to relax at the weekend

Communism

Some of the most famous televised pictures to have emanated from Romania were those of the country's dictator Nicolae Ceauşescu on the balcony of the Communist Central Committee Building in December 1989. Waving to the crowds who had been amassed to show their support for their leader following protests in Timişoara, Ceauşescu's clear shock and incomprehension as they began to jeer him is one of the defining images of the fall of Communism.

Many citizens never dared believe the regime would be toppled. The Communists came to power in 1947. At the end of World War II, the

A stark memorial to those who died in the revolution

leaders of the winning nations, Roosevelt, Churchill and Stalin, met to divide up post-war Europe. Romania was delivered to the Soviet 'sphere of influence'. King Mihai abdicated and went into exile, and the country was declared a Communist People's Republic. The state began to confiscate property, nationalise companies and collectivise farming. One of the most sinister developments was the rise of the Securitate, the Communist Secret Police, who employed an enormous network of informers. Opponents (real or imagined) of the regime were transported or imprisoned. Romania had become a Stalinist state.

When the hitherto obscure Ceauşescu succeeded his former mentor Gheorghe Gheorghiu-Dej as leader, he was initially popular. Appreciated at home for putting more goods in the shops and reining in the Securitate (whose excesses he blamed on his predecessor), he was admired in the West for his independent foreign policy and for being the only Communist leader to oppose the 1968 Soviet invasion of Czechoslovakia, and he was welcomed abroad. Nonetheless, he persisted with the costly

The balcony from which doomed dictator Ceauşescu gave his last public address

industrialisation policy and paying off the foreign debt that financed it, at the expense of feeding his own people. To raise an army of workers, Ceauşescu restricted access to abortion and contraception, and taxed the childless heavily. Discrimination against ethnic minorities was widespread.

Things took a turn for the worse following the dictator's visit to China, North Korea and Vietnam in 1971. Ceauşescu approved of their hard-line Communism, replete with massive civic centres and the near-deification of the leader. Following the trip, he extended his party's powers and stepped up censorship and indoctrination. He kick-started systemisation, an urban planning programme whereby towns and villages were razed to be re-built as Ceauşescu wished. The centrepiece of this was the People's Palace, a huge monolith in downtown Bucharest. The dictator and his wife were venerated in lavish pageants.

All of this did little to distract from the wretched poverty in which the country was mired. Local products (the few that were of sufficient quality) were sold abroad to pay off the national debt. Essentials including electricity, food staples and prescription drugs were restricted. Ironically, it was not this deprivation that prompted the protest that sparked the revolution; instead it was the eviction of a Hungarian priest who had been critical of the regime in the international press. But the demonstration, which started on 16 December in Timişoara, spread throughout the country and culminated, just over a week later, in the show trial and execution of the Ceauşescus. Communism – officially, at least – was finished in Romania.

The Muzeul Naţional de Artă al României

peaceful place to pass a sunny afternoon. The 17-ha (42-acre) facility is home to over 10,000 species of plants, but most locals use the gardens as a park rather than a place to indulge their scientific interest. Keen botanists may wish to peruse the **Botanical Museum**, a Brâncovenesc building near the entrance that contains a thousand exotic plants as well as several thousand of the common or garden variety.
Şoseaua Cotroceni. Tel: (021) 410 9139. www.gradina-botanica.ro. Gardens open: 8am–8pm (summer); 8am–5pm (winter). Museum open: Tue,

Thur, Sat & Sun 9am–1pm. Closed: Mon, Wed & Fri. Admission charge. Metro: Politehnica. Bus: 336.

Grădina Cişmigiu (Cişmigiu Gardens)

In some ways the city's most enchanting green space, Cişmigiu is a favourite with the locals, who descend en masse on summer weekends. The wonderful layout was designed by German landscape architect Carl Meyer. The gardens feel much larger than they are, thanks to the inclusion of separate and distinctive areas that cater to all kinds of park-goer. There's a *Rotonda Scriitorilor* (Writers' Rotunda), a circular section where busts of Romanian literary giants punctuate park benches, invariably occupied by cavorting lovers. Several among the gardens' many monuments commemorate fallen soldiers. A highlight is the lake, for which pedalos and rowing boats can be rented; in winter it is drained and turned into an ice rink. There are several café-restaurants, and the park feels safe and lively well into the night. It's also the one public place when you can sometimes observe a Romanian matrimonial ritual. Bucharest newlyweds love to pose for their wedding photos in the picturesque park (always well tended because it's right opposite the city hall). On warm weekend afternoons during spring and summer, the park is full of wedding parties.

*Bulevardul Regina Elisabeta &
Bulevardul Schitu Măgureanu.
Metro: Izvor.*

Muzeul Național de Artă Contemporană (National Museum of Contemporary Art, or MNAC)

Since its opening in 2004, MNAC has played an active role in Bucharest's arts scene. The decision to house the gallery in Ceaușescu's People's Palace was initially controversial, but the four-level facility with exterior glass lifts has proved to be a modern and remarkable space. The venue showcases multimedia art such as video installations, digital and interactive exhibits. Taking a prompt from the building in which it is housed, the museum also tackles the Communist legacy from time to time. An open-air café on the top floor is a good place to finish a visit.

People's Palace. Strada Izvor 2–4, wing E4 (entrance from Calea 13 Septembrie). Tel: (021) 318 9137. www.mnac.ro. Open: 10am–6pm. Closed: Mon & Tue. Admission charge. Bus: 385.

Muzeul Național de Artă al României (National Art Museum)

Housed in the Royal Palace, former home of the prince under whom Romania's principalities were first

A traditional home at Muzeul Satului

united, the National Art Museum (for some reason never referred to as a gallery) contains Romania's premier collection. The building's three floors each feature one permanent exhibition. The medieval art collection has a predominantly religious theme. Many of the pieces were salvaged from churches around the country and include an impressive 14th-century fresco of the Last Supper. The second-floor modern Romanian art display contains work by all the local masters, the most famous of whom is sculptor Constantin Brâncuşi. European paintings and sculptures also get a floor. A separate wing is home to changing displays by contemporary European artists. The art works are accompanied by informative captions in English. The gallery also hosts some evening events. For more about Romanian art, see the feature later in this guide (*pp94–5*).
Calea Victoriei 49–53. Tel: (021) 313 3030. www.mnar.arts.ro. Open: 10am–6pm. Closed: Mon & Tue. Admission charge. Metro: Piaţa Romană.

Muzeul Satului (Village Museum)

The superlative Village Museum is a microcosm of Romanian architecture, and as such ideal for anyone who wants to get an impression of the whole country without venturing outside Bucharest. The entirely outdoor museum covers 15ha (37 acres) and consists of over 60 original buildings transported from their former locations. Visitors walk around and peer into 18th- and 19th-century houses, churches, mills and farmsteads from all over Romania; a rustic signpost tells you which region is represented where. Some of the buildings have audio information, including in English, available at the touch of a button. There is a well-stocked gift shop and a stall with local produce.
Şoseaua Kiseleff 28–30. Tel: (021) 317 9068. www.muzeulsatului.ro. Open: Tue–Sun 9am–7pm, Mon 9am–5pm. Admission charge, except for visitors with disabilities. Metro: Piaţa Victoriei.

Muzeul Ţăranului Român showcases the bucolic

Muzeul Ţăranului Român (Peasant Museum)

One of the highest-rated museums in the capital and indeed the country, the multifarious exhibits in the Peasant

Museum paint a vivid history of Romanian daily life and customs over last few centuries. Textiles and costumes, pots, carvings, icons and delicately painted eggs are a few of the items on display, and if anything takes your fancy you can usually find a version of it in the museum shop. The basement houses a fascinating and sinister collection of Communist memorabilia – the museum's previous incarnation was as the Communist Party museum – including a portrait of Joseph Stalin and two of Ceauşescu. *Şoseaua Kiseleff 3. Tel: (021) 317 9660. www.muzeultaranuluiroman.ro. Open: 10am–6pm. Closed: Mon. Admission charge. Metro: Piaţa Victoriei.*

The Villacroise passage in Bucharest's Old Town

Old Town

The town's historic centre, sometimes referred to as the Lipscani district, the name of the main street that runs through it, must be one of the most authentic of its kind in Europe. The isolation of Communism and the turmoil of the 1990s allowed the area to develop organically; a district of such ad hoc charm would have been fully harnessed by the tourist industry elsewhere. This is now starting to happen, as trendy (and expensive) cafés join the art, antique and junk shops, but Lipscani retains its chaotic appeal.

In the Middle Ages, it was the most important commercial centre of its principality, and today the streets bear the names of the various traders who plied their wares on them centuries ago. There's little left of the Palatul Curtea Veche (Old Court Palace) itself, but enough of the ruins remain to exude an olde worlde atmosphere, and the Biserica Curtea Veche (Old Court Church), dating from 1545 and the oldest in the city, is still standing. The centre is approximately bordered by Piaţa Unirii to the south, Calea Victoriei to the west and Bălcescu to the east, and extends a little to the north of Strada Lipscani itself. The National Bank building at Lipscani 25 is one of the city's most attractive structures; another is the former CEC bank headquarters on Calea Victoriei 11. *Metro: Piaţa Unirii*

Parcul Herăstrău (Herăstrău Park)

Both the park and its lake of the same name are hugely popular with promenaders, as the large number of cars parked nearby on a weekend will testify. The joggers pounding the path that circumnavigates the lake give the park an international flavour (Romanians are not keen joggers as a rule); so, too, does the collection of top restaurants and trendy lakeside bars. If you want to take to the water – and providing it is between May and September – you can either go it alone, by renting a rowing boat, or do a half-hour cruise. Less appealing is the somewhat rickety fairground.

Metro: Aviatorilor. Bus: 301.

Piața Revoluției

Taking its name from being the location where the Romanian Revolution (which started in Timișoara) erupted in Bucharest, the square is one of the most important and evocative of the city's political history. Many protestors died in the square in the violence that was triggered there, and the authorities have duly made the effort to create a contemplative atmosphere.

Several of the city's most important buildings are clustered here. To the north is the Athénée Palace Hilton, originally designed by French architect Théophile Bradeau between 1912 and 1914. Today a haven of civilised hospitality, its history is more

Have a rest on an inviting bench in Parcul Herăstrău

The *Memorialul Renaşterii*

nefarious. The hotel was a centre of espionage both in the run-up to World War II and the Cold War, and it attracted a phalanx of spies, plotters, plants and prostitutes. The Communists bugged every room after the site was nationalised in 1948. It remained under state ownership until 1994, when it was bought, modernised and expanded by the Hilton group, but the sense of history (if not of skulduggery) has been preserved.

In front and to the left of the hotel is the Athenaeum, beyond which is the former Central Committee of the Communist Party, now ministerial offices, from the balcony of which Ceauşescu delivered his famous last speech. A plaque by the entrance is dedicated to Romania's young revolutionaries. Few cars or pedestrians venture into the area just below the balcony, giving it a somewhat desolate and sombre ambience. There are two memorials to the revolution in this part of the square. One is a traditional marble monument, with the dedication 'Glorie Martirilor Nostri' (To the Glory of our Martyrs). The second is a controversial modern sculpture, *Memorialul Renaşterii*, or the *Rebirth Memorial*, inaugurated in 2005, with what is intended to represent a crown impaled on a 25-m (66-ft) spike. Undeniably eye-catching, it has been criticised for a lack of taste and symbolism. On the same side of the square, between the former Communist Party headquarters and the Ateneul Român, is the Central University

Library, which dates back to 1895 and is now occupied by the European Union. Tucked behind it is the city's most bizarre-looking building. The bottom of it is a derelict-looking shell, the remains of the Securitate (Communist Secret Police) building. An übermodern glass construction has been built within and over it, to house the headquarters of the Romanian Architecture Union. Few other symbols could better sum up Romania's transition.

Directly opposite the ministerial offices and monuments, the other side of Calea Victoriei, which bisects the square, is the National Art Museum in the Royal Palace. To the south of the gallery is the Crețulescu Church, an attractive red-brick building commissioned in 1722, making it among the city's oldest churches.

NICOLAE CEAUSEŞCU

Romania's most notorious president came from humble beginnings as a shoemaker's apprentice. When he first joined the Communists in 1932, the party was illegal. Ceaușescu's agitating and dissemination of anti-Fascist propaganda saw him jailed twice; during his second spell inside he shared a cell with future leader Gheorghe Gheorghiu-Dej. In 1946 he married fellow party member Elena Petrescu, a poorly-educated peasant girl, who would come to exert a Lady Macbeth-like influence over his thinking and policies. Ceaușescu's gradual rise up the party hierarchy saw him succeed his mentor and former cellmate as leader of Romania in 1965, a tenure ended by his trial and execution in 1989.

A blend of Byzantine and Western architecture with local touches, its porch is home to an admirable collection of frescoes from the mid-19th century.
Bus: 126.

Piața Unirii

The heart of Ceaușescu's civic centre, Piața Unirii is a large, flat square, in the middle of which lies a park of sorts (some patches of green flanking a pathway busy with pedestrians trying to make their lengthy way from one side to the other). Permanently teeming with traffic, the square is not the most pleasant place to sit, but there are some attractive fountains and Piața Unirii is a great vantage point for views of the Casa Poporului (People's Palace), which sits imposingly at the end of Bulevardul Unirii. To the north of the square is the Old Town. On the east side is the Unirea shopping centre, with its exterior covered with adverts. There's little of interest to the visitor in it (apart from a few expensive tourist shops on the ground floor), but it is popular with Romanians. The hill that rises from the southwest corner of the square leads to Biserica Mitropoliei (literally, Metropolitan Seat), the Romanian Orthodox cathedral. It's a huge complex, containing frescoes, stone crosses and the Patriarchal Palace. The centre of Romanian Orthodoxy, at various religious festivals it's descended upon by the faithful in droves, and you can sometimes see long, overnight queues of people wanting to touch a relic or perform a devotion.

Metro: Piaţa Unirii. Bus: 104, 116, 123, 124, 232, 312, 385.

BUCHAREST ENVIRONS
Mogoşoaia

Fourteen kilometres (9 miles) northwest of Bucharest and one of the country's most beautiful buildings, the palace at Mogoşoaia was designed by Wallachian Prince Constantin Brâncoveanu. Built at the turn of the 18th century in the Romanian Renaissance style to which the prince gave his name, it features both Venetian and Ottoman aspects.

(Continued p46)

Bucharest

Fountains in Piaţa Unirii, Ceauşescu's huge civic centre

Romanian film

A few years ago, Romania's only role in international film was as a cheap set. Crew wages and location costs were so low that it was cheaper for a Hollywood studio to fly a whole cast over to Eastern Europe than to pay LA rates. The country's adaptable scenery was another draw. A grimy Bucharest apartment block could easily stand in for a run-down New York tenement, and Transylvania for the American South. The latter was the case in Anthony Minghella's *Cold Mountain* (2003), the biggest-budget film shot in Romania.

A quaint old cinema in the capital

Yet recently the country has stopped being known exclusively as a bargain film location and has started making its own waves in world cinema. The 2002 comedy *Filantropica* (*Philanthropy*), directed by Nae Caranfil, collected a few awards at European film festivals. But the first 21st-century Romanian film to get serious publicity was Cristi Puiu's *Moartea domnului Lăzărescu* (*The Death of Mr Lazarescu*), a very black comedy about a dying pensioner who deals with largely uncaring medical professionals as he gets shunted from one hospital to another. It won the Cannes Un Certain Regard prize in 2005, among other awards in Europe and the United States, and garnered much critical acclaim, although the praise was not matched by box office takings.

Much of modern Romanian film concentrates on the legacy of Communism. 2006 saw the release of Corneliu Poromboiu's *A fost sau n-a fost?*, translated as '*12:08 East of Bucharest*', a surreal comedy where the bizarre guests on a talkshow dispute whether the revolution really happened in their town. Life under Communism was also the theme in the most critically successful film to

Film crews are a common sight around Bucharest

emerge from the country. *4 luni, 3 săptămâni şi 2 zile* (*4 Months, 3 Weeks and 2 Days*) from director Cristian Mungiu is the story of two students who seek an illegal abortion for one of them in 1987. The picture debuted at Cannes in 2007, going on to claim the festival's main prize, the Palme d'Or. At the same edition of the festival, *California Dreamin'* by Cristian Nemescu, who was killed in a car crash during post-production on his picture at the age of 27, took the Un Certain Regard award.

The recent successes come despite Romania's lack of tradition of making quality films. Under Communism all cultural output had to serve the propaganda agenda of the state. When a politically independent film did manage to get made, it was banned. Such was the case for director Lucian Pintilie. His feature *O vară de neuitat* (*An Unforgettable Summer*) starring Kristin Scott Thomas, which was nominated for the Palme d'Or at Cannes, is credited as inspiration for the new generation of flourishing filmmakers.

But Romania's filmic achievements in its own right have not stopped foreign crews using the country for budget filmmaking. The most controversial example of late was when British comedian Sacha Baron Cohen picked the small village of Glod to represent Kazakhstan in the film *Borat*. The villagers took such umbrage at their depiction that they sued the film company. The lawsuit was thrown out.

The Orthodox monastery of Snagov is a UNESCO World Heritage Site

Destroyed by the Russians in 1853, it was rebuilt in the 20th century by an Italian architect. The museum to which some of the house has been given over is not the most inspiring, thanks in large measure to Ceaușescu, who co-opted much of the original furniture for his own use, but there are a few artefacts of note. More striking is the Communist 'graveyard' north of the house, where dumped statues of Lenin and erstwhile Romanian Prime Minister Petru Groza lie abandoned to the weeds.

A visit to the palace could be combined with Snagov (*see below*) on a day trip if you have your own transport, although it is not on the same road. Whatever your plans, it is better to drive or take a taxi in terms of flexibility and timing, but you can reach Mogoşoaia on public transport if that is your preference. *Strada Valea Parcului 1, Mogoşoaia. Tel: (021) 350 6619 or (021) 350 6620. Open: Tue–Sun 10am–6pm (summer); Tue–Sun 9am–5pm (winter). Closed: Mon. Admission charge for grounds and for museum. Bus: 460 from Laromet.*

Snagov

Hugely popular with weekenders from Bucharest, Snagov lies just 40km (25 miles) north of the capital. Fortunately, its best part, the monastery, is of little interest to most of the day-trippers, and visitors will often find that they have the place to themselves. Part of the reason for this is its isolation; it's on an island, reachable by hired boat (self-rowed or manned) from a jetty about 1.6km (1 mile) north of the village of Snagov, next to Complex Astoria. The 16th-century church is a UNESCO World Heritage Site, and the headless body of Vlad Ţepeş is said to lie just below the dome. Dracula's burial place is surprisingly simple and tranquil, the grave marked by a solitary portrait.

Less tranquil are the water sports that take place on the 16-km (10-mile) long lake, where speedboat trips, kayaking, waterskiing, jetskiing and banana boating are possible. In winter, the lake is sometimes turned into an ice

THE CHEEKY GIRLS

Twin sisters from Cluj, the Cheeky Girls, Monica and Gabriela Irimia, found fame as contestants on the British TV talent show *Popstars*. Despite failing to reach the final stages (and harsh criticism from the judges), the novelty of the sister act garnered them notoriety and the twins received several offers from record companies. Their first single *The Cheeky Song (Touch My Bum)*, written by their mother, who is also their manager, reached number 2 in the UK charts in December 2002. Just over a year later it was voted the worst pop record of all time in a poll. Despite poor reviews, the sisters continue in the limelight, especially since Gabriela began dating politician Lembit Öpik.

rink. The area also has a little-known wildlife reserve south of the lake. It is home to protected flora and fauna, and deer, pheasants and owls are among the potential sightings.

Noteworthy buildings in the vicinity include the 19th-century Snagov Palace and Villa Number 10, Ceauşescu's summer house. However, most local visitors come simply to relax, enjoy a barbecue, swim and sunbathe. Weekends at Snagov can get exceptionally busy, so if you appreciate peace and quiet it's best to visit on a weekday.

Snagov is most easily reached by car or taxi (although the latter could be pricy unless you're travelling in a group), public transport options being limited to bus.
Monastery open: daylight hours. Admission charge for monastery. Bus: 444 from Piaţa Presei Libere.

The Latin element

Romania is proud of its status as the only Latin country in southeast Europe, wedged between Slavic nations. Although it has a few words from its neighbours' tongues, the vast majority of its language is directly traceable to Latin. This certainly helps foreign visitors, whose school-level French can prove useful in deciphering signs and simple texts. Its Latin roots come from the 2nd-century Roman invasion of what was in those days known as Dacia, when the local people adopted the language of their conquerors.

Dacia, ancient Romania, could be seen as a victim of its own success. The end of the 1st century saw the peak of the Dacian civilisation, and it came to be seen as a potential threat to the Roman Empire. The two sides waged war against each other. Julius Caesar had first wanted to invade the land, but was assassinated before he got the chance. Emperor Trajan subsequently led the invasion, and Dacia came under Roman occupation for more than 150 years. But Barbarian tribes also had Dacia in their sights and the Goths eventually ousted the Romans.

A century and a half may not seem a particularly long period in the formation of a nation, but it was a defining one for Dacia. The area benefited from the various advancements with which the Romans became synonymous. Agriculture, mining, trade, art and culture all developed and advanced significantly thanks to Roman intervention. As well as the language, the other main legacy from the conquerors was Christianity. Later, even the country's name would reflect its brief spell of Roman occupation, although the area of Dacia did not come to be officially known as Romania for centuries. The association is one the local people like to advertise, through such means as the Romulus and Remus statue at Piața Romană, the square's name itself obviously also paying testament to the country's Latin origins.

Today's Romanians exhibit many of the traits popularly thought of as Latin. They are a demonstrative people, emphasising their points with dramatic gestures. Comfortable with physical closeness, they kiss each other hello and goodbye, regardless of gender. Female friends also hold hands as they walk along the street. The chaotic driving associated with Italy and Latin America is also replicated in Romania, where failure to hoot enough seems to be interpreted as a sign of weakness. And while the country's economic and political situation has never allowed the people to develop the style of their Italian and French counterparts, Romanians enjoy getting dressed up and take pride in their appearance.

The Latin link has great bearing on the countries to which Romanians generally choose to emigrate. Two of the top destinations are Italy and Spain, where Romanians can get by in the local language and feel at ease with the culture. Melodramatic Latin American soaps, *telenovelas*, have huge followings in Romania, which now produces domestic versions. The country also has a particularly strong relationship with France, which goes back centuries, and in 2006 hosted the 11th Francophonie Summit.

The Latin influence on Romania can be seen in its architecture

The Prahova Valley

The Prahova Valley, Sinaia in particular, is the holiday and weekend destination of choice for Romanians from the capital and throughout the region. While it is briefly overshadowed for a couple of months in the summer, when thoughts turn to the beach, it retains a steady flow of visitors throughout the year. The Bucegi mountains are the main draw, but the Prahova river also makes a contribution to the stunning scenery, in what is one of Romania's most beautiful areas.

The valley itself carves out the journey from Wallachia to Transylvania, and was historically important as the passageway between these two principalities. The route is still considered a vital one; it is part of the A3, currently the largest highway project in Europe, which will run from Bucharest to Oradea, close to the Hungarian border.

The county (judeţul Prahova) is one of Romania's most populous, with over 800,000 citizens. The valley itself marks the division between the southern end of the Eastern Carpathians and the Bucegi mountains. Although parts of the county are made up of plains, it is the four main mountain resorts – Sinaia, Buşteni, Azuga and Predeal – that attract the most visitors. Extraordinary caves, stunning waterfalls, rock formations and man-made monuments are among the highlights of the mountains, accessible to hikers and mountain bikers. The resorts' position on the main road between Bucharest and Braşov undoubtedly helps. There is

Detail of Castelul Peleş

a relaxed, almost provincial, pace of life in all four resorts.

A car affords the easiest way to explore the Pravoha Valley, allowing you to nip easily between the towns, which are all close to each other, and ascend some of the mountains without relying on the cable cars, which sometimes close due to the weather or lack of demand. (Obviously common sense and possibly tyre chains are useful if you're driving in mid-winter.) But it's perfectly possible to visit the resorts using public transport. Frequent fast trains from Bucharest's Gara de Nord stop at Sinaia and Predeal, where you can change to pick up a slow train to Buşteni. Avoid the *personal* train, which takes three hours, twice as long as the fast option. Travel between the resorts is possible by bus, maxi-taxi or cab.

Azuga

Lying at the foot of the Bucegi mountains, Azuga's main claim to fame is a brewery that churns out the eponymous beer. The town's connections with alcohol go back some way; the Rhein Azuga cellar became an official supplier to the royal family in 1920. It now hosts wine-tasting for tourists, and even offers accommodation. Azuga's other chief attraction is the longest ski run in the country, known as Sorica. The other ski run, Cazacu, has artificial snow machines. A nursery slope caters to beginners. Azuga (*www.ski-in-romania.com*) is a relatively new ski

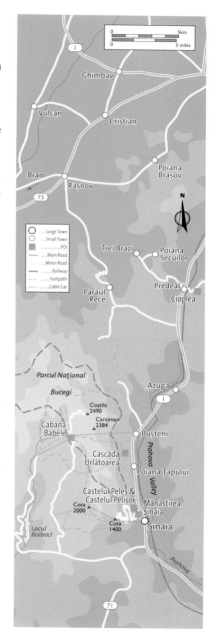

resort and facilities are being gradually built up to meet demand from skiers. *Rhein Azuga cellar. Strada Independentei 24. Tel: (0244) 530 955 or (0244) 326 560. Open: Mon–Fri 8am–4.30pm, Sat & Sun 10am–4.30pm (and by appointment after hours for larger groups who also want dinner). Admission charge.*

Bucegi mountains

The dramatic Bucegi mountains, covered in a dense carpet of trees, offer some of the best mountain terrain and views to be had throughout Romania. Geared up for hikers, there are plenty of trails, marked by a system of coloured signs, as well as cabanas, popular with skiers too. Mountain bikers can follow some, but not all, of the trails as well. Along with the natural highlights on show, mankind has also had some creative input into the area. Ialomiciora Monastery, built inside a cave, is one example.

If you're serious about hiking it is worth purchasing a reliable map of the region. Also, be warned that the mountains can suffer from harsh weather. If the wind gets up, the chair lift or cable car will be stopped, even if passengers are still on it. The delights of the spectacular mountain views can pale rather quickly when you've been dangling on a chair lift in the cold for half an hour. The Bucegi mountains, while practically unheard of outside the country, are famous throughout Romania, and in peak season things can get pretty busy, with long queues for lifts.

Buşteni

The town itself has a couple of places of interest, namely the house and memorial museum of writer Cezar Petrescu (*Tudor Vladimirescu 2. Tel: (0244) 321 080*) and a 19th-century church. But Buşteni's main draw is as a base from which to explore the

Architecture takes on an alpine aspect on the way into Transylvania

A roadside market at the entrance to Sinaia offers a motley collection of wares

surrounding areas and the highlights of its two imposing peaks, Caraiman and Coştila, 2,384m and 2,490m (7,820ft and 8,170ft) high, respectively. Its small-town feel (it is home to 15,000 people) belies a tumultuous history; the mountains and town were the scene of hostilities during World War I. The 25-m (82-ft) high *Crucea Eroilor* (*Heroes' Cross*) on Caraiman Peak, at an altitude of about 2,260m (7,415ft), commemorates the loss of life. Lit up at night it can be seen from the town. The cross is just one of the distinctive mountain features. The pretty Cascada Urlătoarea (literally, 'Screaming Waterfall', giving an indication of the noise it makes), the prominent rock formations Babele şi Sfinxul (The Old Women and the Sphinx), and the Cascada Moara Dracului (Devil's Mill

Waterfall), whose dramatic name is well suited, are a few of the sights accessible to hikers. Anyone prepared to do some serious walking can even walk from here to Bran.
Cable car. Tel: (0244) 320 306.
Open: 8am–3.45pm.
Closed: Tue.

Predeal

Romania's highest town, lying at an altitude of 1,033m (3,390ft), marks the point where Wallachia gives way to Transylvania. A good starting point for walks, it is also a ski centre, and there are places to hire equipment during ski season. Most serious skiers, however, stick to the resorts further south, or head straight to Braşov, as Predeal's slopes are not as long or as exciting as those of its neighbours. Perhaps for this reason, it has a quieter feel. A combination of ozone-rich air and low pressure are said to be curative of medical conditions including exhaustion.

Sinaia

The former royal retreat of Sinaia is the first Prahova Valley resort on the road from Bucharest to Braşov and the most impressive. Like the other towns in the area, the action is centred on and around the main road that bisects the resort. Many of the small interconnecting roads set back from the large thoroughfare are joined by sets of steps, and climbing is likely to be a feature of your stay. The town was named after its monastery, which took its own name from the Biblical Mount

MIORIŢA

The pastoral ballad of Mioriţa, or The Little Ewe, is one of Romania's most enduring folk tales. The story starts with three shepherds, a Moldavian, a Transylvanian and a Vrâncean. One day, the ewe tells the Moldavian that his two fellow shepherds are planning to murder him and divide up his flock. Rather than outwitting the conspirators or making his escape, the shepherd asks the ewe only to ensure that his body is buried by his sheep pen. Instead of telling his mother the truth, the ewe is to say the boy married a princess. Commentators link the fatalistic tale with love of the land, nostalgia and Christian principles.

Sinai. Thanks to the town's status as the summer residence of King Carol, several of the buildings here are of a high aesthetic standard. Other sights include the following:

Castelul Peleş brings some royal glamour to the Prahova Valley

A typical mountain chalet in Predeal

Castelul Peleş (Peleş Castle)

A dazzling palace that is rightly held up as being one of the most beautiful in Europe, Peleş is the most spectacular man-made construction in the Prahova Valley. Built at the end of the 19th century, around the time that Romania became a kingdom, it was to serve as summer residence for the new king. A neo-Renaissance building, it had input from German and Czech architects. The result is a castle that would not look out of place in a fairy story, with towering turrets and landscaped gardens in the English tradition. Overall, the architects and interior designers drew inspiration from a mélange of styles, including Renaissance, neo-Renaissance, baroque, Moorish, Florentine and rococo.

Some of the 160 individually decorated rooms can be visited on a 40-minute guided tour (solo exploration is not allowed), for which you must cover your shoes with special slippers to protect the flooring and carpets. The tour takes in various halls, nooks and crannies including the weapons room, king's study and council room. The range of different aesthetics on display is remarkable. Sadly, the ageing wood of the upper levels does not permit visitors to see above the ground floor. Peleş proudly holds the record of being the first European castle to be entirely lit by electrical current.

Aleea Peleşului, Sinaia. Tel: (0244) 312 184. Open: Wed–Sun 9am–5pm,

Tue 11am–5pm. Closed: Mon.
Admission charge.

Castelul Pelişor (Pelişor Palace)

Though it would be immensely
impressive anywhere else, Pelişor is
somewhat eclipsed by its grander
neighbour Peleş Castle, which also has
a German Renaissance-style exterior.
Another royal residence, Pelişor, which
means 'Little Peleş', was intended for
the king's nephew Ferdinand, who
would later succeed to the throne.
Ferdinand's wife Marie was given the
task of choosing the furniture; she went
for art nouveau pieces, many of which
were from Vienna. A little distance past
Pelişor is Foişor Lodge, which can
only be viewed from the outside.
Aleea Peleşului, Sinaia. Tel: (0244)
310 918. Open: Wed–Sun 9am–5pm,
Tue 11am–5pm. Closed: Mon.
Admission charge.

Cota 1400

The 1,400-m (4,590-ft) altitude point,
known as Cota 1400, is a stop-off point
on Sinaia's mountainside. It can be
reached either by cable car or by car,
up a 8-km (5-mile) road, some of
which is in poor condition. Bears
occasionally venture close to the road,
where they are fed by motorists who
stop to take pictures. The practice
might incur the wrath of biologists
(bears overly used to human contact

This distinctive Sinaia landmark is still a working
monastery

MEŞTERUL MANOLE

A typically fatalistic Romanian myth, the
story of 'The Master Builder Manole' is
connected to the Cathedral of Curtea de
Argeş in southern Romania, which Manole
and some fellow builders were working on.
The legend has it that the construction walls
kept collapsing, threatening the completion
of the project. The builders decided to make
a sacrifice, and that the first woman who
came along would be bricked, live, into the
wall. While the other workers warned their
wives not to bring them lunch that day,
Manole's dutiful wife turned up on time, and
was imprisoned in the wall for her pains. The
construction was thence completed.

have attacked people in the past), but it inarguably results in some great photos. There is not very much at Cota 1400 itself, aside from hotels, cabanas, ski hire outlets in winter and a couple of places to eat. Visitors tend to park here to take photos of the wonderful scenery or have a bite to eat while enjoying the mountain view.

Cota 2000

The serious action takes place at the 2,000m (6,560ft) point, which you reach by cable car from Cota 1400. In winter, hardcore skiers start from here on their challenging route back to the bottom of the lift. Hikers also set off from this point, and from the slightly lower Cota 1950, with coloured signs marking out a circular path. Routes are available for walkers of every energy level, from gentle half-hour strolls to full-on treks back down the mountain. Depending on which you take, look out for caves, gorges, waterfalls and natural bridges en route.

Cable car. Tel: (0244) 311 872.
Open: 8.30am–4 or 5pm.
Closed: Mon (all year), if weather is bad (windy), or if demand is low.
Admission charge.

**Mănăstirea Sinaia
(Sinaia Monastery)**

The monastery, which retains its air of peace and contemplation despite the many tourists traipsing around, was built at the end of the 17th century. The site consists of two churches, the newer

Quintessentially Romanian spires and mountains

and more prominent of which is a mid-19th-century neo-Byzantine addition. The inside is dark, dominated by large amounts of gold and chandeliers. To the right as you enter is a museum housing a display of religious artefacts, a small shop can be found inside the church, and there is also a pretty bell tower.

The older church was built in 1695 by the monks who had inhabited the mountains since the 14th century. Next to it lies the tomb of Tache Ionescu, who briefly led the country in the 1920s.

Strada Mănăstirea, Sinaia. Open: daylight hours. Admission charge.

Drive: the Prahova Valley

This 40-km (25-mile) drive will open up some of Romania's most dramatic mountain scenery. The marvellous views can be enjoyed from the car, but you will get more out of it if you take the time to make a few stops and explore on foot; at the very least, you'll enjoy oodles of bracing mountain air.

The journey can be done in a day, but you may prefer to spread it over two for a more leisurely pace.

Start at Sinaia (120km/75 miles from Bucharest on the DN1 road). Take a left (assuming you are coming from Bucharest) into Strada Aosta then turn right into Strada Cantâcuzino. When you reach Strada Mănăstirea turn left. The road bends sharply twice before you will see the monastery on your left.

1 Mănăstirea Sinaia

The functioning monastery is home to around 20 monks (*see p57*).
From the monastery, continue along the road in the same direction you were travelling. The road merges with Aleea

Cioplea has many mountain chalets, some of which are hotels

Peleşului, which leads to Peleş Castle. You will have to park in the pay carpark here, as only official cars are allowed right up to Peleş and Pelişor.

2 Castelul Peleş

The tour of this glorious former royal residence (*see pp55–6*) takes about 40 minutes, but you should leave over an hour for the steep climb to the castle, waiting time for the tour, and a few minutes to take photos of the exterior, which you will definitely want to do.
Continue up the hill for about 200m (219 yds) until you see the second palace.

3 Castelul Pelişor

Though clearly outshone by Peleş, the smaller castle has plenty of glamour of its own (*see p56*).
Return to your car and head back the way you came. The first main right leads to Cota 1400, a 16-km (10-mile) round trip; there are signs if you get lost. Another option is to park your car

*by the cable-car station by Strada Cuza
Vodă, and take the cable car.*

4 Cota 1400

With its marvellous views, this place is
ideal for a panoramic lunch or a brief
mountain stroll (*see pp56–7*).
*Head back down the mountain and
rejoin the main road, travelling in the
same direction as before. The next town
you reach will be Buşteni. The cable
car is on the left-hand side,
immediately after you enter the town;
ride it up to Cabana Babele.*

5 Babele şi Sfinxul (The Old Women and the Sphinx)

These two famous rock formations
carved out by the wind are said to
resemble an old woman and a face
respectively. There are plenty of great
hikes and bike rides that can be done
from this spot in the Bucegi mountains.
*Come back down and carry on along
the main road to Predeal. Right before
the stadium turn right onto Bulevardul
Libertăţii. The road winds round the
stadium and bends again sharply to the
left. Follow it for another few minutes
and you will reach Cioplea.*

6 Cioplea

The excellent views at Cioplea are set
off by beautiful mountain chalets. You
can rent a quad bike and explore the
forest, or head back down Bulevardul
Libertăţii and round the day off at one
of the decent restaurants at the southern
end of the street.

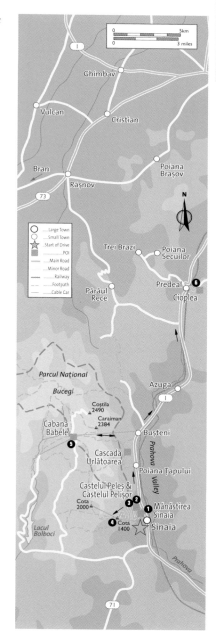

Drive: the Prahova Valley

Skiing

Romania's harsh winters – the bane of much of the rest of the population – are ideal for skiers. The mountain resorts often get snow from the end of November to the end of March, sometimes as late as April. While the infrastructure may not be as classy as you'd get in the Alps, and the *après-ski* essentials (decent hotels, restaurants and bars) still suffer from the Communist customer service ethic, this is more than compensated for by the prices; skiing in Romania represents some of the best-value

piste action in Europe. And things are gradually improving in the services department too.

As yet, Romania's only international-standard resort, and the only one frequented by major external holiday companies, is Poiana Braşov in Transylvania. Not only are its ski facilities up to scratch – it has 12 slopes, including an Olympic run – but it is close to the tourist town of Braşov, ensuring that there is plenty to do off piste.

Elsewhere, standards vary. The lift man may bundle you rather than help you off the lift. If you don't have your own equipment, what you are able to hire may be slightly shabbier than what you'd find in other countries. In Romania, 'the customer is always right' is not a creed many hold dear. Many business owners mistrust their customers and you will be commanded to leave your ID (probably your passport) while you have the skis to ensure you don't run off with them. The hotels and restaurants in resorts may also be rather dispiriting. Although most of the ski resorts have one black-graded run, the majority are suited to beginners, so expert skiers may become bored. (The exceptions are

Whether you like cross-country skiing...

...or challenging slopes, Predeal is popular with skiers

the challenging slopes at Caraiman and Coştila.)

But authorities from other areas of the country are now waking up to the fact that their mountains represent a huge, untapped resource. A national, government-backed plan is being rolled out to help mountain resorts meet their full ski potential. Investments are being made in facilities such as artificial snow machines and gondolas, as well as in road and airport improvements. Tourism in Romania is developing across the board, and service is also getting better.

The best argument for skiing in Romania at the moment is definitely the cost. Cheaper skiing is hard to find anywhere in Europe. Courses can cost less than 50 lei per day, ten trips

on the lift about the same. The advent of cheap flights, which started in response to the European Union's approval of Romania's EU membership, have reduced the previously prohibitive cost of reaching the country from Western Europe, making Romania a viable destination for a long weekend of skiing. Romanians, too, are keen skiers, and at weekends resorts can get packed, with long queues forming at the bottom of ski lifts. If too few people show up, the operators may choose not to run the lift at all, however, so going midweek can also be risky.

The best-known resorts are in the Prahova Valley and Poiana Braşov, but there are resorts spread throughout the country, including the Făgăraş mountains for long-distance ski treks.

Transylvania

Without doubt, Transylvania is the most famous part of Romania, as much thanks to Irish authors and American film producers as to its own authentic characteristics. However, the movie version of a dark place of creepy castles and howling wolves is not entirely mythical. The densely wooded Carpathian mountains are home to some of the largest European wild carnivore populations outside Russia, not to mention underground rivers, caves and other striking natural phenomena.

On top of the dramatic scenery that lends itself so easily to Hollywood, the other thing that marks Transylvania as different from the rest of the country is its ethnic make-up and history. Until as late as 1918, the region was not even part of Romania, but was Hungarian territory. Prior to that it had been variously part of Dacia, the Roman Empire, the Hun Empire, and Gepid (controlled by the Goths); it was autonomous under Ottoman suzerainty and came under Habsburg control. Disputes over 'ownership' have continued well into the 21st century, with some voices still calling for independence. Some Transylvanian settlements are home to more ethnic Hungarians than Romanians, and you will hear Magyar spoken frequently. Food served up here usually has more in common with

Red roofs stretch off into the distance in a classic Transylvanian panorama

spicy Hungarian fare than the blander Romanian version.

Many towns have also played host to occupying Saxons, and although the majority of the descendants of the original families have now left, their influence remains in the prettily coloured houses and fortified churches. The third significant ethnic group is the Roma. Unlike in other parts of the country, where they largely blend in with the local population, Transylvanian Roma are distinctive thanks to the ten-gallon hats sported by the men and the ornate gypsy dresses of the women.

The colourful ethnic mix is a huge part of Transylvania's appeal to tourists. Here, the Latin commotion that accompanies most simple activities elsewhere (the aggressive hooting of drivers, the rush to board buses and the metro, the volume of normal conversations) is tempered, and life is lived at a calmer, less frenetic pace.

The Saxon architectural and cultural legacy, showcased at its best in cities like Sibiu, seems to have brought with it some refinement, and such towns often seem closer in spirit to Germany and Austria than Romania. Add to that the natural attractions of the mountains, with their quirky grottos, sheer massifs, meandering paths for walkers and cyclists, the occasional bear spot and other happy surprises, and it is little wonder that Transylvania is high on any tourist's to-do list.

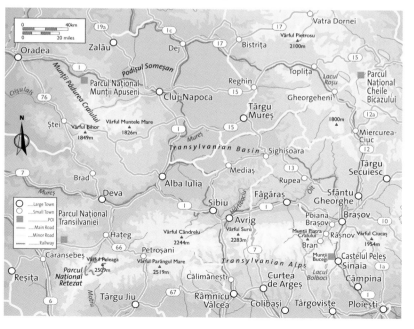

Braşov

It's neither the largest nor the most populous town in Transylvania, but in the public consciousness Braşov is certainly the capital of the region. The town, brimming with picturesque baroque architecture, is many visitors' first stop in Romania outside Bucharest. This is partly because Braşov in itself is a lovely, laid-back place to pass a few days, with some of the best cultural and culinary options outside the capital. It also makes a convenient base for day trips to smaller sites such as Bran.

Situated 166km (just over 100 miles) north of Bucharest, Braşov lies north of the chain of resorts that makes up the Prahova Valley, and is considered by many Romanians as the entrance to Transylvania. Relaxed and peaceful, it is hard to believe that in the 1950s the town was renamed Oraşul Stalin, or Stalin Town. The Hollywood-style sign (with viewing platform) in Mount Tâmpa now simply reads Braşov, but even that feels out of place and self-promoting in a town more given to low-key charm.

The main action centres on Piaţa Sfatului, a large pedestrianised square containing several historical buildings, and bordered in the main by cafés. On warm days local students and tourists pass their time on terraces, overlooking the modern fountain display. Leading into Piaţa Sfatului is Strada Republicii, also closed to vehicles and similarly abundant in places to stop for a coffee and a snack. Boutiques are quite common in these areas, and the shops have mostly adapted their frontages to suit the old-fashioned atmosphere.

COMMUNIST JOKES

There may have been little to laugh at during the deprivations of Communism but throughout Romania and the Eastern bloc a rich vein of humour developed as an antidote to everyday woes. In the climate of censorship and surveillance by the authorities, jokes were mini-rebellions, a way of debunking the regime's propaganda and pomposity. *Securitate* officers had to file reports of political jokes, which were illegal, as a means of keeping tabs on the mood of the nation. Few gags were laugh-out-loud hilarious in their own right. Instead, they spoke of Communist absurdity and misinformation, and made light of daily travails. 'What is colder in a Romanian winter than cold water?' goes one joke. 'Hot water!'

Biserica Neagră (Black Church)

Construction of this large Gothic church began in the 14th century. Despite its name (conferred following a fire in 1689), it is bright inside. Features include impressive front columns, Ottoman carpets and attractive wooden carvings. Most impressive is the huge organ at the back, said to consist of 400 pipes. Organ recitals are held on Tuesdays at 6pm in summer (tickets can be bought at the church); the schedule is subject to change. The back of the building houses a gallery with stone wall carvings, displays of old prints from religious texts, photographs and maps. You can also buy postcards and books.

Piaţa Sfatului. Open to visitors: Mon–Sat 9am–6pm. Services: Sun 8am–11am or noon. Admission charge.

Poarta Ecatherinei (Catherine's Gate)

The Upper Gate, as it is sometimes known, was designed to facilitate access to a medieval fortress, of which the outer tower is still standing. Built in 1559, it bears the town's coat of arms, and is now surrounded by gardens. Don't get it confused with Poarta Şchei, immediately to the east, which was the toll gate for the poor Romanian speakers who were exiled to outside the citadel under Saxon rule and had to pay to get in.

Off Strata Poarta Şchei.

Poarta Ecatherinei was once the city's main entrance

Walk: central Brașov

Brașov's old-town feel is facilitated by its size; all the main attractions are within walking distance of each other. Most of the highlights are either historical or religious in character, but some recreational options have been added too.

Allow two to three hours.

Start in Piața Sfatului.

1 Catedrala Ortodoxă (Orthodox Cathedral)

This Byzantine-style church, built at the end of the 19th century, is a reproduction of the Greek Church in Vienna; it contains the usual quota of impressive frescoes and interior design.
Walk southwards across Piața Sfatului. The Black Church is in front of you.

2 Biserica Neagră (Black Church)

This large Gothic church (*see pp64–5*) brings home the differences in style between Orthodoxy and the Lutheran faith.
From the Black Church, take the road on the left which joins Strada Poarta Șchei. Turn right on Poarta Șchei.

3 Synagoga (Synagogue)

Large and bright white with stained-glass windows, the neo-Roman/Moorish design was the work of an

Austrian Jew, Leopold Baumhorn.
Open: Mon–Fri 9am–1pm. Outside the synagogue turn left. Pass under Poarta Șchei and turn right into the small park.

4 Poarta Ecaterinei (Catherine's Gate)

This 16th-century gate was part of a medieval fortress (*see p65*).
Leave the park by the opposite side. Cross over the road, and take the second right onto Strada După Ziduri.

5 Bastionul Fierarilor, Turnul Negru, Turnul Alb (Blacksmiths' Bastion, Black Tower, White Tower)

These buildings remain in excellent condition considering the pounding the town took from the Tartars, Turks and Vlad Țepeș. The Blacksmiths' Bastion today houses a collection of old and rare documents, including the oldest letter ever written in the Romanian language. The 9-m (29-ft) Black Tower, which, like the Black Church, is not black, houses a tiny collection of war memorabilia.

The White Tower is a 200-step climb up the hill. It is slightly taller than its black counterpart, at 14m (46ft). *Rejoin Strada După Ziduri and walk away from Catherine's Gate. At the end of the road, turn right onto Bulevardul Eroilor.*

6 Parcul Central

The well-kept park, popular with Braşov's chess-playing fraternity, is a pleasant place for a sit down. *Rejoin Bulevardul Eroilor, and walk left to Piaţa Revoluţiei. The road to your right is Strada Republicii.*

7 Strada Republicii

Choose one of the street's many coffee houses and restaurants in which to recuperate.
The end of the street brings you back to your starting point.

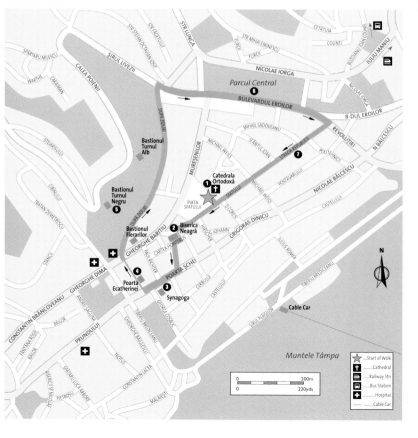

Tâmpa (Mount Tâmpa)

To the east of the town is Mount Tâmpa. It's possible to go up the mountain by cable car; the station is up some stairs from Strada Romer. You can also make the fairly undemanding climb on foot; marked by red triangles, the winding trail takes about an hour. You'll no longer be able to see much of the town's original defensive fortress – Vlad Țepeș dismantled it and impaled 40 people for good measure – but the peak affords fantastic views over the red roofs of the city and the surrounding mountains. At the foot of Tâmpa, close to the cable-car station, the remains of the old city wall have been undergoing renovation.

Bran
Castelul Bran (Bran Castle)

One of the top tourist attractions in Romania, although Vlad Țepeș's (unproven) connection with the castle is that he might have once spent a few nights there. The structure's resemblance to the Hollywood version of 'Dracula's castle' is such that it has been hijacked by the Dracula industry – evidenced by the huge swathe of Vlad and vampire merchandise on sale at the market outside, from wine to masks to swords to coffee mugs. Bran certainly has the spooky turrets, the hilltop position and the dense forest surroundings to give a passable impression of a vampiric hideaway, but

Bran Castelul fulfils many Draculaphiles' expectations of Transylvania

in daylight its red and white exterior has a pleasant, not remotely threatening aspect.

There are castle tours in English, but they do not adhere to a regular programme. When you turn up, you may attract the attentions of a guide. Typically young and male, their wry commentary includes lines such as 'Count Dracula likes to drink the blood of young virgins; you will all be safe'. The tours are free but the guides appreciate a tip. You will see the pleasant courtyard with its well, narrow staircases and various rooms, each with at least a few pieces of furniture. The ticket to Bran Castle also includes entry to the site's village museum.

The castle has been the subject of legal wrangling between the Romanian state and a New York architect, Dominic Habsburg, the grandson of the former occupier Queen Marie. Seized by the Communists in 1947 and opened to the public, in 2006 the castle was awarded to Habsburg. The architect said he would sell it back to the Romanian state, but since then arguments have sprung up over his asking price and the legality of the whole process. The site should remain open to the public, but check before you go if it's an important part of your trip.

Strada Traian Mosoiu 489, Bran.
Tel: (0268) 238 333.
www.brancastlemuseum.ro. Open: Mon noon–6pm, Tue–Sun 9am–6pm (May–Sept); Tue–Sun 9am–4pm (Oct–Apr). Admission charge.

The region is full of mountain roads

Cheile Bicazului (Bicaz Gorges)

Some of Romania's most dramatic mountain scenery can be found at the 8-km (5-mile) long Bicaz Gorges, which have been carved into the Jurassic limestone of the Hăşmaş massif by the Bicaz river. The gorges connect Transylvania and the region to the east, Moldavia. Driving through them, along the Transfăgărăşan road, the country's highest asphalted route, is an extraordinary panoramic journey. The so-called Gâtul Iadului (Throat of Hell) consists of overhanging rocks, under which local artisans, attracted by the relatively high numbers of tourists, ply their trade. At this point the road is

Matei Corvin personifies the region's
Hungarian links

feel rather than the atmosphere of a
bustling metropolis. The students also
ensure a lively nightlife. Founded on
the site of a Roman legion camp, the
town was settled by the Saxons in the
13th century, and still retains its
historical air. Almost one fifth of the
population is Hungarian, and the
divisions are more evident here than
elsewhere, with distinctive education
and cultural institutions. While most
other towns of its size went under the
bulldozers of Communist town
planners, Cluj avoided that fate and has
kept many of its old structures, albeit
in a deteriorated state, and all within
walking distance of each other.

shaped straight from the rock face
itself, and the sunlight is blocked,
leaving the river that runs through the
site in atmospheric darkness.

Striking heights, known by
Romanians as *pietre* (stones), rise
dramatically from the landscape. The
gorges, among the deepest in the
Carpathians, pull in serious rock-
climbing enthusiasts keen to take up
the challenge of 300-m (985-ft) rock
faces, ceilings and cracks. To a lesser
extent, the area is also good for
twitchers, who get excited about the
resident Eurasian eagle owl. The
gorges are part of a protected area.

Cluj–Napoca

The largest town in Transylvania is
also home to the country's largest
university, which gives Cluj a casual

Grădina Botanică Alexandru Borza (Alexandru Borza Botanic Gardens)

Europe's largest botanical gardens
stretch over 14ha (34 acres) and feature

ȘTEFAN CEL MARE

Somewhat overshadowed by his more
notorious contemporary Vlad Țepeș, Ștefan
cel Mare, or Stephen the Great, spent almost
half a century as the Prince of Moldavia, a
region which would later correspond
approximately to northeast Romania. Under
his leadership, the state saw off attacks from
Hungary, Poland and the Ottoman Empire,
but it was his resistance to the latter that won
Stephen his country's enduring regard. The
prince triumphed in 34 of his 36 battles, and
was declared a *verus christianae fidei athleta*
(true champion of the Christian faith) by the
pope after becoming the first to achieve a
crucial victory over the Turks. His victories
are commemorated by the legacy of the
churches he built.

10,000 species of plant. Fauna from all the Romanian regions are represented, and there are also greenhouses containing plants from tropical regions. The Japanese garden is particularly pretty. There is also an observation tower.
Strada Bilaşcu/Republicii 42. Tel: (0264) 592 152. www.cjnet.ro. Open: 9am–7 or 8pm. Admission charge.

Muzeul Naţional de Artă Cluj (Art Museum)

One of the most important art collections in the country, the predominantly traditional exhibits include works by Nicolae Grigorescu, Theodor Aman and Theodor Pallay. It is housed in the Bánffy Palace, an 18th-century baroque building by German architect Johann Eberhard Blaumann. Occasional events are held in the courtyard.

Piaţa Unirii 30. Tel: (0264) 596 952. Open: Wed–Sun noon–7pm (June–Oct); Wed–Sun 11am–6pm (Nov–May). Admission charge.

Muzeul National de Istorie a Transilvaniei (National History Museum of Transylvania)

This sizeable museum, a century and a half old, has permanent exhibitions on the prehistoric, Dacian, Roman, medieval and modern periods, plus a display on Egyptian history. There are also temporary exhibitions. Among the most notable exhibits are the remains of three corpses thought to be Indo-Europeans.
Strada Constantin Daicoviciu 2. Tel: (0264) 591 718. www.museum.utcluj.ro. Open: Tue–Sun 10am–4pm. Closed: Mon. Admission charge.

Its university gives Cluj a laidback vibe and thriving cultural and social scene

Wildlife

Romania may not be the first country that springs to mind for a wildlife holiday. But it has two important wilderness zones, which have been more or less left alone by humans. The Carpathian mountains, thick with fir trees, provide a people-free haven for various large carnivores, while the Danube Delta is bursting with avian, aquatic and plant life. There are easy opportunities for close encounters with such creatures for the merely curious; enthusiasts can dedicate whole trips to their animal passion, with the help of specialist companies and associations.

There is a limit to how much humans can encroach on the second most extensive mountain system in Europe. The result is that parts of the Carpathians are remote enough for several animal populations to have flourished; the Romanian section of the range is said to be home to almost one third of all European large carnivores. About 2,000–3,000 wolves, driven to extinction in many other European countries, live in Romania's forests. It is possible to track these shy creatures on specialist holidays. Unfortunately, not everyone tracking them is an awed and respectful tourist; although the animals are protected by law, limited hunting is allowed.

Slightly easier to spot than the wolf is the bear. Romania has plenty of the creatures, almost 60 per cent of Europe's entire population, it is said. Brown bears are found particularly in the Eastern Carpathians. It was once

Some brown bears are losing their shyness around humans

common for tourists to roll up in minibuses or taxis to the Racadau suburb of Braşov, where bears regularly descended to rummage through the neighbourhood bins. Since a rabid bear killed two people in 2004, the authorities have tried to clamp down on the practice. However, some bears are quite used to humans and approach mountain roads, where they are often fed by drivers. Bears are hunted to a small degree.

The final member of Romania's 'big three' is the lynx, a big cat, which escapes a great deal of human attention, probably because its better-known and larger cousins tend to take the limelight.

During the tribulations of post-Communist Romania, animal rights were far down the list of most people's concerns, but the country is now starting to realise what an asset and tourist draw its wildlife could be. Projects such as the Carpathian Large Carnivore Project, which ended its ten-year span in 2003, attempt to promote knowledge and conservation of the species.

The country's other main wildlife refuge is the Danube Delta, a twitcher's paradise due to its location on the major avian migration route that runs from east Africa to the Arctic. Of the 300 species who pass through at some point, some breed, others stop off, and others hunker

Birdlife is abundant in the Danube Delta

down for the winter. Even low season is rich in birdlife, although enthusiasts time their trips for the avian 'rush hour'.

The Delta is, if anything, even more abundant in plant life, with over 1,600 different species. The same is true of the Carpathians, some of the flowers here being endemic. The best floral displays are to be found between April and July. Romania's varied climate and geology offer a varied selection of other fauna.

Piaţa Unirii

This square has undergone several politically inspired name changes between its current title and Piaţa Libertăţii (Freedom Square). The nationalist theme is further in evidence with the commanding statue of Hungarian King Mátyás Corvinus (Matei Corvin in Romanian) on horseback trampling the Turkish banner. Even more imposing is the 14th-century Biserica Sfântul Mihail (St Michael's Church), held by many to be among Romania's best Gothic buildings.

Lacul Roşu (Red Lake)

Despite its olde-worlde mystical atmosphere, the Red Lake is a comparatively recent addition to the Romanian landscape, having been formed in 1837–8 by a landslide which dammed the River Bicaz. Just the other side of the Transylvanian–Moldavian border, the lake derives its moniker from the reddy sediment that the main tributary river, Piriul Roşu (the Red Creek), deposits here. A grislier legend attributes it to the blood of picnickers supposed to have been crushed by the mountain. The lake, which has a surface

Lacul Roşu is distinctive for its protruding tree trunks and gory creation myth

area of 12.6ha (31 acres), is 10.5m (35ft) deep.

Its most distinctive feature – which lends it a rather eerie aspect – are the fir tree trunks that protrude, some straight upright, others at jaunty angles, from the water. The effect is almost as if there were some sort of city under the water. The background of dense pines adds to the sense of seclusion. The Hungarians have recognised the inherently sinister atmosphere, calling the lake Gyilkostó, which translates to 'Murderers' Lake'.

Miercurea-Ciuc

Visitors planning to reach Miercurea-Ciuc in winter should take heed of its reputation as the coldest city in Romania. Perhaps insulation is one reason behind the locals' love of the eponymous beer, Ciuc. The town is a major point in Székely Land, an ethnic Hungarian region deriving its name from the Magyar minority living in central Romania. Four fifths of its population are ethnic Hungarians. Although much of the town's Habsburg architecture was destroyed by the Communists, the citadel and a few other buildings of note remain.

The county capital of Harghita lies 100km (62 miles) north of Brașov in the Olt Valley. The large student population gives Miercurea-Ciuc a youthful feel, and a decent selection of cafés, bars and restaurants has burgeoned to cater to it; many of the

The pretty church towers of Miercurea-Ciuc

eateries have a Hungarian flavour. Whit Sunday, seven weeks after Easter Sunday, sees a couple of hundred thousand worshippers descend on the city for the Székely pilgrimage, a tradition which began in the 16th century. Dressed in black, they sing and queue to touch a statue at a local Franciscan monastery.

Cetatii Mikó (Mikó Citadel)

The town's top landmark, the 17th-century Mikó Citadel was built on the foundations of the original castle erected in the 11th century and destroyed by subsequent wars. Not as overtly martial in aspect as many, it was intended as a fortified residential palace rather than a military facility.

The Transylvanian countryside has many peaceful landscapes

What currently stands dates mainly from 1714 when the site was rebuilt by the Habsburgs. The building houses the Székely Museum of Csik, a small collection of local weapons, costumes and artefacts. Outside are some examples of local architecture.
In between Piaţa Cetatii & Strada Eroilior. Tel: (0266) 311 727. Open: Tue–Sun 9am–5pm. Closed: Mon. Admission charge.

Poiana Braşov

Tiny Poiana Braşov, 12km (7½ miles) southwest of Braşov, is most famous outside the country as a ski resort, at the time of writing the only one regularly used by foreign tour operators. In the usual Romanian style, everything centres on the road that runs through it.

There is also a lake, which is nice enough but not among the country's prettiest. Quad bikes can be hired to explore the surrounding forests. The place tries to retain an old-town feel, with traditional restaurants (the kind that display stuffed animal heads on the wall) dotted about. Braşov is near enough for anyone who wants more sophisticated cuisine or nightlife.

Biserica Sfântul Ioan Botezătorul (Church of St John the Baptist)

The most prominent sight in Poiana Braşov is Biserica Sfântul Ioan Botezătorul. Its wooden design is a copy of the traditional Maramureş style, but the structure is in fact relatively new. Its spire goes up some way but the church itself is small inside, and rustic rather than ornate. The painted scenes have an almost comic-book simplicity about them. At the back, a friendly priest sells jewellery, icons and CDs from a desk. Outside, there is a place down some steps where visitors can light a candle.
Open: 8am–9pm. Free admission.

Cable car

The cable car at Poiana Braşov theoretically runs all year round, although it may be closed from time to time if the weather is bad, say, or the operators anticipate low demand. Even if you're a non-skier, the eight-minute (each way) journey is worth it for the views.
Open: 9am–4 or 5pm in summer. Admission charge.

Sibiu

Once overshadowed by Braşov and Sighişoara, Sibiu, to the west of Braşov, now has a persuasive claim to have the nicest city centre in Romania. This is mostly thanks to the town's selection as 2007 European Capital of Culture (joint with Luxembourg), which resulted in a raft of improvements and cultural events. Founded in the 12th century by German settlers, the town has a Saxon aesthetic and calm Germanic atmosphere that lend it a very un-Romanian feel.

(*Continued p82*)

The church Sfântul Ioan Botezătorul recalls the Maramureş style

Drive: Braşov–Râşnov–Bran

Few visitors to Braşov leave without having seen Bran. Its reputation as Dracula's castle is now too well established for anyone to be concerned about the fact that the man spent a day or two there at most. This 50-km (31-mile) drive makes a scenic day trip, taking in other places of interest and panoramic spots en route.

From Braşov, take the road DJ101H to Poiana Braşov, which is well signposted. Slightly before the 4-km (2¹/₂-mile) mark are three photo stops, one after the other, on the left-hand side. Pull over here.

1 Braşov

The panoramic mountainside position affords beautiful views of the red roofs of Braşov, Mount Tâmpa and its huge Braşov sign, and the mountain's dense coating of trees.
Continue on the road to Poiana Braşov.

2 Poiana Braşov

Famous as a ski resort, the small hamlet is equally pretty in summertime. Its most eye-catching structure is the lovely wooden church of Sfântul Ioan Botezătorul (*see p77*) on the left side of the road. On the opposite side is a lake.
Turn round and drive back the way you came. At the entrance to Poiana

Braşov is a left turn. Take it and follow signs to Râşnov.

3 Râşnov

The fortress at Râşnov sees fewer tourists than Bran Castle, probably because pedestrians are deterred by the 15-minute climb (or more, depending on your level of fitness) required to reach it. If you want some exercise, the steps start at Piaţa Unirii in Râşnov town. Drivers can take the road up the hill. The ruined 13th-century fortress, originally built by the Teutonic Knights to help defend themselves from the Tartars, has now been partially restored. The grounds include a jail and a church, and there's a small museum with weapons and other medieval artefacts.
Cetatea Râşnov (Râşnov fortress). Tel: (0268) 230 255. Open: 9am–8pm (summer); 9am–5pm (winter). Admission charge. Carry on driving until you reach Bran and its castle.

4 Castelul Bran

So-called 'Dracula's castle' may have little connection to the count – or even to his real-life inspiration – but exploring this Saxon castle, with its narrow stairways, medieval knick-knacks and grand European furniture (much of which is the original stuff) is still plenty of fun (*see pp68–9*).

From Bran, take the road signposted for Câmpulung. At Moieciu de Jos, a dirt track forking off to the right leads to Peştera.

5 Peştera

The village's name means 'cave', and the chief attraction here is the 160-m

(525-ft) long bat cave, part of which can be visited.

Free admission.

Back on the Câmpulung road, continue for another 10km (6 miles) to Fundata.

6 Fundata

One of the highest villages in Romania on the Bran or Giuvala Pass, Fundata affords superb views of rolling hills and distant cliffs, tiny farms, a rustic ambience and an annual summer festival.

You can head back to Bran or you could stay in one of Fundata's pensions.

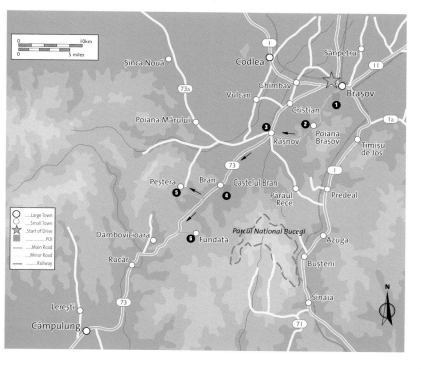

Dracula

Romania's number one cultural association was little known in the country itself prior to 1989. The myth was built on the shakiest of grounds, fusing a brutal Romanian prince with an entirely unconnected fictional vampire. The two were combined by an Irish writer, Bram Stoker, who never went to Romania but pieced his plot together with maps and timetables at the British Library. This has not stopped a huge Dracula cult developing, a vampiric cash cow for Hollywood and Romanian tourism.

Stoker's choice of the Wallachian prince Vlad Țepeș as the inspiration for the antagonist of his book seems to have had at least some rationale. Țepeș was sometimes called Dracula, the name being the diminutive version of his father's name, Dracul, meaning 'the devil' or 'the dragon'. The 15th-century prince has been accused of cannibalism, but historians give little credence to the allegations. Aside from a name, the two villains share a reputation for brutality and strength. Țepeș managed to hold the Ottomans at bay for some time (for which he is remembered warmly in Romania) and Count Dracula is said to have 'the strength of 20 men'.

Hollywood was quick to spot the potential of the Dracula myth. Early examples were the 1922 silent film *Nosferatu* and 1931's *Dracula* starring Bela Lugosi. Starting in 1958, English actor Christopher Lee starred as the vampire in a string of Hammer Horror films, and the cinematic fascination continues, with *Bram Stoker's Dracula*, *Van Helsing* and *Dracula 2000* among the more high-profile

The wonderfully camp Count Dracula Club is a tourist must-see

Vlad the Impaler was the inspiration for Count Dracula

'Dracula's castle', where the man himself may have spent a night or two. The so-called 'real Dracula's castle' is Poienari Citadel in Argeş Valley, Wallachia, which Ţepeş had captured Turks build for him. In the book, the count lives near Bistriţa. Things should wind up at Snagov, just north of Bucharest, where Ţepeş's headless body is said to lie.

The actual sites are accompanied by a slew of mostly tacky Dracula souvenirs, including hosts of vampiric masks, and even a brand of wine called Vampire (red, of course). Some venues really camp it up. Bucharest's Count Dracula Club (see p149) is a themed restaurant, with a menu based painstakingly on Bram Stoker's novel. Twice a week, to a soundtrack of howling wolves and creepy music, a Dracula impersonator goes from table to table, scaring diners, and performs a hilarious show.

recent features to draw inspiration from the character.

At first bemused by the West's obsession with this fictional creation, Romania has now also started to reap the rewards as Dracula enthusiasts flock to Transylvanian castles. A proper Dracula trail, done chronologically, should start in Sighişoara, home to Casa Dracula, a pizza restaurant built on the site where Vlad Ţepeş was born. Next stop Bran Castle, known by many as

Some of the worst excesses of Dracula mania, though, have been tempered. A mooted theme park, Dracula Park, attracted opposition from everybody from the Romanian church to Prince Charles. After five years of changing venues, squabbling and newspaper articles about 'the idea that just won't die', the plan now seems to have been shelved, although the Dracula Park website hopefully states that 'draculapark.ro is coming soon'.

The town centre is comprised of three picturesque, cobble-stoned squares, Piaţa Mare, Piaţa Mică and Piaţa Huet, and cafés, restaurants and terraces are in plentiful supply. Even the normal high-street stores and banks have eschewed their usual shop fronts and insignia for something more old-fashioned and in keeping with the Sibiu ethos. Everything is near to everything else, making this a great walking town. There are enough fascinating buildings, including charming pastel-coloured Saxon homes, to delight casual strollers, but many buildings merit a visit inside.

Sibiu has a relaxed, Viennese feel to it

Sibiu is particularly strong on culture. Churches, museums and galleries dominate the cityscape. The city hosts annual jazz and international theatre festivals, and there is also a range of evening entertainment, from jazz and classical music to theatre.

Catedrala Evanghelică (Evangelical Cathedral)

A towering presence in the square, the Gothic cathedral is the town's centre of the Lutheran faith, although the building was previously used by Catholic worshippers. Its dimensions and plain stone give it an atmospheric and imposing air. The enormous church organ at the back is the largest in the country. The tomb of Dracula's son is, appropriately, in the crypt (viewable upon request); he was stabbed to death outside the cathedral after Mass. A World War I memorial is among the collection of monuments. The seating section is roped off, with a warning to beware of falling stones. If you have energy for the nearly 200-step climb, the church tower affords marvellous city views.

Piaţa Huet. Open: Mon–Sat 9am–8pm, Sun 11am–8pm. Admission charge.

Galeria de Artă Contemporană (Contemporary Art Gallery)

Part of the Brukenthal, this new gallery, opened in March 2007, is housed in a lovely old building. It currently hosts temporary exhibitions

Be sure to tell the truth on Podul Minciunilor (Liar's Bridge)!

by European artists, including graphic art, photos, videos and sound installations. The site is something of a work in progress, with the ultimate aim being to move the modern exhibits from the Brukenthal (*see below*) to here, leaving the latter exclusively for traditional art.
Strada Tribunei 6.
www.brukenthalmuseum.ro. Open:
10am–6pm. Closed: Mon. Free
admission, but subject to change.

Muzeul de Etnografie şi Artă Populară Săsească Emil Sigerus (Emil Sigerus Ethnography Museum and Saxon Folk Art)
A bright and cheerful museum with colourful rustic furniture and just one main room. The gallery has a small shop.
Piaţa Mică 21. Tel: (0269) 218 195.
www.muzeulastra.ro/emilsigerus.
Open: 10am–6pm. Closed: Mon.
Admission charge.

Walk: Sibiu Old Town

With so many monuments and buildings of note and beauty in such a small space, it would be difficult to walk in central Sibiu without passing sundry places of interest. The town's Germanic olden-day charm lends itself to strolling, and there is always a welcoming café nearby when you need a sit down.

Allow two hours at a relaxed pace.

Start in Piaţa Mică, the northernmost of the three squares that make up the old centre.

1 Turnul Scărilor (Staircase Tower)

Built in the 18th century, the mustard-coloured tower looks down on a 13th-century passageway. Standing underneath it gives a great glimpse of Strada Movilei with its medieval turrets and cobblestones.

Facing the square, bear to the right.

2 Podul Minciunilor (Liar's Bridge)

Romania's oldest cast-iron bridge, built in 1859, takes its curious name from the legend that anyone who stood on it and told a lie would cause it to collapse. The two swords and crown imprinted on it were the emblem that indicated Saxon acceptance of Hungarian and Transylvanian jurisdiction.

South of Liar's Bridge is the Evangelical Cathedral.

3 Catedrala Evanghelică (Evangelical Cathedral)

This cathedral is distinctive for its massive church organ and tall tower, visible from all over town and beyond. The view from the top merits the demanding climb.

On the opposite side of Piaţa Mică is Turnul Sfatului.

4 Turnul Sfatului (Council Tower)

The gate below this tower provides access between Piaţa Mică and Piaţa Mare. Built in the 13th century, restored after a 16th-century collapse and extended in the 19th century, it has been variously used as a jail and a corn storehouse.

Walk south through Piaţa Mare and take Strada Mitropoliei; walk 200m (218yds).

5 Catedrala Ortodoxă (Orthodox Cathedral)

Built at the start of the 20th century, the second largest Orthodox cathedral in Romania stands on the former site of a Greek church and was designed by Hungarian architects. The domed neo-Byzantine interior hosts a huge gold chandelier as well as colourful frescoes. *Continue down the road in the same direction. After about 150m (164yds) you will reach Astra Park on your left.*

6 Parcul Astra (Astra Park)

Fountains, and statues of the Romanian great and good, are the main focal points in this pretty park, whose tree-lined pathways have benches for a pleasant seat in the sunshine. *Leave the park by the opposite side, turn left and walk until the intersection. Turn right. Climb the set of steps ahead, leading to Bulevardul Corneliu Coposu. Turn left.*

7 Old wall

Walking down the boulevard you will have a view of the remains of Sibiu's fortifications, including its defensive towers.

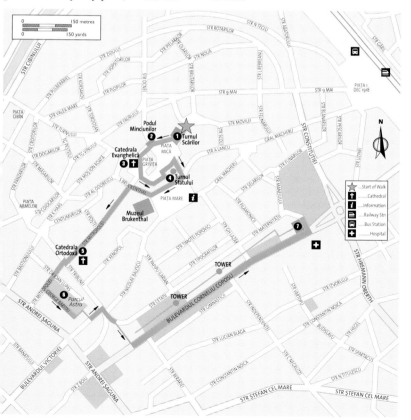

The citadel harks back to medieval times

Palatului Brukenthal (Brukenthal Palace)

Set around a pleasant courtyard, the baroque Brukenthal Palace houses an excellent collection of art in suitably palatial rooms, some of which contain original rococo furniture. Many exhibits have inscriptions in English. Works include Renaissance paintings of the German, Austrian, Italian, Spanish, Dutch and Flemish schools. Local and religious art is also well represented, as are modernism and sculpture. The gallery would be quite at home in any major European city.

Piața Mare 4–5. Tel: (0269) 217 691. www.brukenthalmuseum.ro. Open: 10am–6pm (summer); 11am–5pm (winter). Closed: Mon (all year). Admission charge.

Sighișoara

Dracula's/Vlad Țepeș's celebrated birthplace is similar to the other major Saxon cities in Transylvania; speckled with cobbled streets and charming Saxon houses that form part of a tiny town centre surrounded by the remnants of a medieval citadel. Sighișoara is even smaller than Brașov, Cluj and Sibiu, and with fewer international-standard dining options and cultural events it tends to be a shorter stop on most tourists' Transylvanian trail. None the less, its historical attractions are up there with the best of them.

Less encroached upon by the tell-tale signs of modernisation, Sighișoara's centre certainly exudes a highly atmospheric and mythical charm, added to by the slightly rugged German cemetery. The area inside the city wall is barely 250m (820ft) in diameter at its widest point. Dotted around the wall is the usual collection of historical towers. North of the old town, the Târnava Mare River winds its way.

Biserica Mănăstirii (Monastery Church)

Once the property of the Dominican monastery, and now a Lutheran place of worship, the Gothic-style Monastery Church has been rebuilt several times since its inception in the 13th century. Highlights include the bronze frontage, vivid 17th-century Eastern carpets and a baroque organ, sometimes used in recitals. Behind the church is a statue of Vlad Țepeș.

*Piaţa Cetatii. Open: Mon–Sat
10am–6pm, Sun 11.15am–6pm.
Free admission.*

Camera de Tortura (Torture Room)

A tiny but gruesome museum in the room where doomed prisoners in the Middle Ages were brought to have their fingers smashed or feet crushed, or suffer other, similarly horrible fates. One such unfortunate soul in the 17th century carved the German for 'Tomorrow I will be…' into a brick; the last word is obscured.

Situated in the History Museum (see listing below for details of opening times). Admission charge.

Casa Dracula (Dracula's House)

In typically low-key Sighişoara style, the mustard-coloured, three-storey house on the site where Dracula came into the world has been given over to a run-of-the-mill restaurant, which, apart from the name, does little to celebrate the legend. A wrought-iron dragon (*dracul* means 'dragon' as well as 'devil') hangs above the door. Although the building is indeed historical, it has been entirely rebuilt since the days when it was home to the toddler Ţepeş.

Strada Cositorarilor 5. Tel: (0265) 771 596. Open: 10am–midnight.

Muzeul de Istorie (History Museum)

Housed inside the clock tower that dominates Sighişoara's old town, the exhibits are spread through seven small rooms, one above the other. The museum affords a good chance to get up close to the city's famous clock, out of which come two sets of rotating wooden figures. Day, night and the days of the week are indicated by the goddesses of peace, justice and fairness, and the Roman gods. Elsewhere in the quirky museum there are displays on space pioneer Hermann Oberth, Transylvanian crafts, Renaissance furniture, medical implements and, appropriately enough for a clock tower, a selection of clocks.

Piaţa Muzeului 1. Tel: (0265) 771 108. Open: Mon 10am–6pm, Tue–Fri 9am–6.30pm, Sat & Sun 9am–4.30pm (mid-May–mid-Sept); Tue–Fri 9am–3.30pm, Sat & Sun 10am–3.30pm, closed Mon (mid-Sept–mid-May). Admission charge.

The Sighişoara clock also tells the days of the week

Ethnic minorities

On arrival, Romania does not seem an ethnically diverse country. Black and Asian visitors still attract stares, even in the cities, and many local people share a homogeneous Mediterranean-cum-Balkan appearance, with dark hair, slightly tanned skin and brown eyes. However, several distinct ethnic groups can be observed, and when you reach certain parts of Transylvania

A symbol of Romania's multi-ethnic history

such differences are a defining part of life. In some areas, minority languages have special status and their own educational and cultural institutions.

The most numerous minority population (6.6 per cent, or around 1.4 million people) in Romania is Hungarian. In two counties, Harghita and Covasna, they form the majority. Magyar communities are mostly based in Transylvania, previously part of Hungary, and represent a fifth of its people. But the Magyar presence is not solely due to Transylvania's change of ownership. Nomadic tribes settled in what is now Moldavia as early as the 8th and 9th centuries, leaving only during a Mongol invasion. A Hungarian Roman Catholic community later settled in the same area. Magyarisation policies in the 19th and 20th centuries were intended to consolidate Hungarian control over the area.

The Entente powers' decision to return Transylvania to Romania after World War I prompted an exodus of Hungarians. Those who remained lost land, saw their language erased from official life and place names, and faced other discrimination, a process which was continued, after a brief hiatus, by the Communists. But the

The striking interior of Braşov's synagogue

border. Among them were members of the religious order of the Teutonic Knights. After the order was expelled by the king of Hungary, some remained and a Saxon community developed. In time, many Saxons left for Germany, many more after World War II. However, with almost 0.3 per cent of the population, they remain a significant presence in some areas, and have left an impressive architectural legacy.

First documented under the Roman regime, the tiny population of Romanian Jews began to grow around 1850, reaching 12 per cent of the total population by 1859, and grew again in the interwar period, considered Romania's golden age. As elsewhere in Europe, 20th-century harassment variously took the forms of loss of suffrage, violence, synagogue desecration, forced expulsion and exclusion from schools. After World War I, Romania agreed to emancipate the Jews, but the rise of Fascism in the 1930s and advent of World War II put paid to that, and the Jews suffered horrendously in the Holocaust, a situation only recently addressed by the Wiesel Commission in 2003. While many Romanian Jews left for Israel, the situation is now much improved for the 10,000 or so remaining.

The Roma are explored in more detail on pp114–15.

prospect of the two countries being part of a common body – the European Union – improved relations. The Democratic Union of Hungarians in Romania, the political party set up after the Romanian Revolution, has been well represented in government for more than a decade, and Hungarian schools, media, cultural and educational institutions have proliferated.

The Saxons also played a key role in Transylvanian development. They started to settle in the region in the 12th century, when the Germans colonised it, and were tasked with defending Hungary's southwest

Northern Romania and the monasteries

Travelling in northern Romania often makes you feel as though you've gone back in time. Without Bucharest's thirst for modernisation and the West, and without Braşov's legions of tourists and the Dracula industry, the north of the country is possibly the closest you will get to medieval life anywhere in Europe. Peasant culture is still surviving here, and traditional costumes are the normal attire.

This preservation of heritage is thanks in part to the area's geographical and geological characteristics, cut off as it is by the Carpathians on one side and the Ukraine on the other. This isolation has had several effects. Ceauşescu did not overly concern himself with the remote north country (largely unsuitable for farming, it did not get subsumed by his collectivisation policy), and Communism did not leave the profound scars here that it did elsewhere. The lack of external influence here also allowed superstition and religion to flourish. This spirituality generated what is probably the area's chief draw, namely the dozens of picturesque monasteries and churches, many of which date back centuries, and most of which are in excellent condition.

Two of the three northern counties dealt with below have populations around the average; Suceava is home to a little under 700,000 people, and the population of Maramureş numbers over 500,000. Satu Mare, parts of whose perimeter border both Ukraine and Hungary, is less populous with around 370,000 residents.

Maramureş

The name can refer both to the county of Maramureş, and to the wider valley region that extends into Ukraine.

A typical church in Câmpulung Moldovenesc

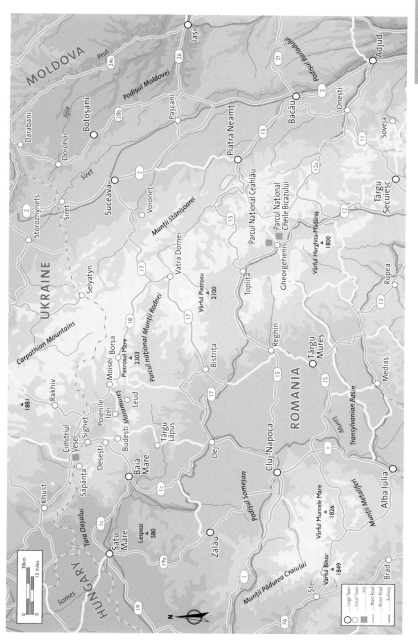

Northern Romania and the monasteries

A Maramureş woman occupied with traditional handicrafts

In common with much of the rest of northern Romania, Maramureş is a rural idyll for travellers keen to get off the beaten track and away from the tourist hordes. The pastoral and agricultural traditions of the region continue, unchecked by the Communist industrialisation, and it is common to see peasants tilling the land in the same way as their forebears did in bygone ages. The area's most famous asset is its wooden churches.

Cimitirul Vesel (Merry Cemetery)
Joyous rather than solemn, the extraordinary Merry Cemetery is dotted with bright wooden headstones, painted with portraits and scenes from the deceaseds' lives. The poetic inscriptions, if you can find someone to translate them for you, are often uproariously irreverent. One reads: 'Here lies my mother-in-law / Had she lived another year / I would be lying here.' Another runs: 'Burn in Hell you damned taxi / That came from Sibiu / As large as Romania is / You couldn't find any other place to stop / Only in front of my house / To kill me?' The scene above pictures the victim and the fatal taxi. The stones are the work of woodcarver Stan Ion Pătraş and, since his death in 1977 (Pătraş painted his own cross), his apprentices. There's a small museum on the site, too.
The cemetery is in the village of Săpânţa, 16km (10 miles) northwest of Sighet.
Săpânţa. Open: daylight hours.
Admission charge. Bus: from Sighet
(weekdays, once daily) or Bogdan Voda
(weekdays, twice daily).

Vasser Valley Railway
Built in 1925, the narrow-gauge railway transports timber the 42km (26 miles) between Vişeu de Sus and the logging camp near the Ukrainian border. Steam trains still operate on the route, although they are being phased out to make way for diesel engines. Tourists can make the same journey on a train that runs once a day, leaving at 8.30am and returning at 5.30pm. In summer the route can also be hiked.
Gara CFF Vişeu de Sus. Strada
Carpaţi. Tel: (0262) 353 535.
Admission charge.

Wooden churches

The wooden churches owe their existence to the area's centuries-old tradition of logging – and to the 1278 Catholic-imposed interdiction on building churches from stone. They were mostly built in the 17th and 18th centuries on the sites of older churches that had not survived the fighting in the area.

The approximately 42 Orthodox churches, 8 of which make up a UNESCO World Heritage Site, are typically narrow and high. Their tall clock towers, some of which reach 50m (164ft), are at the western end; the churches face eastwards. Inside they are usually small and dark, with 18th- and 19th-century wall paintings combining religious and pagan motifs with a topical bent. The sites are sometimes locked up, and you may have to ask around to track down the person with the key. Dress conservatively and refrain from smoking. The eight UNESCO churches can be found in Bârsana, Budeşti, Deseşti, Leud (home to the oldest church), Sisesti, Poienile Izei (which boasts dramatically hellish frescoes), Târgu Lăpuş and Sisesti.

The extraordinary Cimitirul Vesel has an unusual take on death

Art

If it is hard to picture a style of art that could be considered distinctively Romanian, that is probably because local art is a mélange of external influences, which reflects the country's patchwork history of foreign intervention as well as its own preoccupations. Not only did external trends inform Romanian styles, but many of the country's artists – in line with its intellectuals – left their homeland to study their craft in Europe. Two big names in world art,

Dan Perjovschi's work packs a political punch

Nicolae Grigorescu and Constantin Brâncuşi, were such exiles.

In the Middle Ages, much art was of a religious bent, intended to instruct illiterate peasants and to rouse soldiers before battle. In the Byzantine style, it consisted of frescoes of Biblical scenes, displayed both inside and on the exterior walls of churches. A colourful and often extremely well-preserved legacy remains in Bucovina, in the northeast of the country, and Maramureş. While the techniques that enabled the paintings to survive for centuries were highly efficient, the artwork itself is stylistically naïve, often resembling comic-book-style narratives. This reflects the lack of formal education of the artists, as well as the simple, rustic lifestyle of the area.

Later, in the 19th century, influence came from the West, with local painters absorbing and regurgitating what they had seen in Western Europe, in particular France. The big name of the time was Nicolae Grigorescu (1838–1907), considered the founder of modern Romanian painting. Although he left at a young age to study in Paris, he did not turn his back on his homeland, and returned several times, even serving as a frontline painter in the Romanian War of Independence against the Ottomans. The themes of his work were largely pastoral, consisting of peasants, horses and carts, and rustic landscapes. The two Paris-educated Theordors, Aman (1831–91), a portraitist and pioneer of Impressionism, and Pallady (1871–1956), whose work referenced Symbolism, Renaissance and Cubism, were other key figures.

But the only artist to rival Grigorescu in stature was sculptor Constantin Brâncuşi (1876–1957). His revolutionary style made him a founding figure of modern sculpture. The ostensible simplicity of his works, such as the *Infinite Column* on display in a park in Târgu Jiu, conceals a complexity of thought, and his creations are on show today in major museums and galleries around the world.

Art under Communism consisted of nothing more controversial than dreary still-life and Socialist-Realist paintings venerating the Communist élite; anything more challenging was suppressed. Following the revolution, the sudden freedom of expression and influx of foreign ideas brought about a period of great experimentation and a new generation of questioning and political artists, such as Dan Perjovschi, whose unpretentious line-drawings satirise local and global political issues.

The Brukenthal in Sibiu has one of the country's best collections of art

The precocious Cubist painter and muralist Alexandra Nechita, who left the country at the age of two for the United States, is an atypical figure on the scene. Having had her first exhibition, in Los Angeles, at the age of eight, she earned the nickname 'the petite Picasso'.

Romania has a plethora of galleries (mostly known as art museums), but the most cutting-edge are confined to the big cities.

Traditional hats are still the norm in parts of the north

Satu Mare

Satu Mare, the westernmost of
Romania's northern row of counties,
borders both Hungary and Ukraine.
Ruined fortresses bear testament to its
troubled history, but it also has the
usual assortment of churches and
monuments. Farming is a significant
part of the economy, and traditional
peasant ways have been maintained,
just as they have elsewhere in the
north. Its sizeable Hungarian
contingent, slightly over a third of the
population, can be found mainly
towards the border.

While its tourist lures are not as
obvious as those of Maramureş and
Suceava, the counties to the east, the
relative rarity of visitors to Satu Mare
can be a bonus, as locals will be even
more surprised and pleased to find that
foreigners wish to visit their home. The
landscape, which generally flattens out
as you travel from east to west through
Romania's northern counties, is
rustically pretty and the county makes
a good stop-over for anyone wishing to
continue their journey to Hungary. Its
main claim to fame is as the origin of
the Satmar, a community of Hasidic

Jews who can now be found in New York, London and Jerusalem.

Oraşul Satu Mare (Satu Mare City)

While it is not Romania's most attractive city, the county capital Satu Mare is a developed town in which to get back to civilisation after forays into the Romanian countryside. There is quite a bit by way of culture, including a large art museum, the **Muzeul de Artă**, which showcases the work of mainly local artists, and the Muzeul Judeţean, or county museum, which has archaeological and ethnographical displays, including traditional rural costumes and ceramics.

Amid the largely dreary Communist architecture are a few real gems. On the northern side of Piaţa Libertăţii is the Hotel Dacia, formerly the city hall and royal court. A glorious Secession-style edifice, it was built in 1902 to the winning design of a Vienna architecture competition. On the eastern side of the same square is the bright 18th-century Roman Catholic Cathedral, a neo-classical building extensively restored after sustaining damage in World War II.

Muzeul de Artă. Intersection of Strada Cuza Voda & Piaţa Libertăţii. Tel: (0261) 710 114. Open: Tue–Sat 10am–6pm, Sun 10am–2pm. Closed: Mon. Admission charge.

Muzeul Judeţean. Strada Vasile Lucaciu 21. Tel: (0261) 737 526. Open: Tue–Fri 9am–5pm, Sat 9am–4pm. Closed: Mon. Admission charge.

Tara Oaşului (Oaş Country and mountains)

Delineated by Turţ-Gherţa Mare-Gherţa Mică to the west, Huta pass in the east, Cămărzana above and the mountains to the south, Oaş Country is a geographical depression in the east of the county. It is host to one of Romania's quirky rural festivals, Sâmbra Oilor (the Gathering of the Sheep), which gives the mountain-bound sheep a good send-off, and sees cheese and wool divided among the owners and shepherds. It is marked with music and dancing by participants in traditional costume.

The whole area has a rugged feel to it, and most villages lie alongside the river valleys. The volcanic Oaş Mountains, part of the Eastern Carpathians, are another tourist draw.

The 18th-century Roman Catholic Cathedral

Suceava

Romania's second largest county is the gateway to southern Bucovina (the northern part is in Ukraine), famous for its 48 painted monasteries, 7 of which are UNESCO-protected. Along with Maramureş, Suceava is one of the country's most unspoiled rural areas. The dense woods of the Carpathians spread this far north, and the region's hilly topography affords the visitor enchanting views. Scenes are flecked with rustic cottages, haystacks and the odd horse and cart.

The lack of development does have one obvious disadvantage; getting around the region without your own transport can be difficult. The monasteries are often in remote locations, and only some are served by bus. Taxi drivers are sometimes willing to negotiate a fee for a day's travelling. Another option is hitch-hiking; although this is generally considered safe, the usual considerations apply.

Oraşul Suceava (Suceava City)

The city has suffered from Communist industrialisation, but can serve as a well-placed base for touring the local monasteries. It also has several notable churches of its own. Worth seeing are the Byzantine St Dimitru's Church, next to the market on Strada Curtea Domneasca, the Mirăuţi Church, the city's oldest, on Strada Mirăuţilor, and the Monastery of St John the New, east of Piaţa 22 Decembrie.

Painted monasteries

Some of Romania's true treasures, most of the monasteries and Byzantine churches are almost immaculately preserved from the 15th and 16th centuries. Painted, sometimes inside and out, they boast vividly coloured Biblical scenes and religious imagery. Most of the monasteries were built by Ştefan cel Mare (Stephen the Great), the second most famous Romanian

Haystacks dot the Romanian landscape

prince after Dracula, to commemorate his victories in battle. Fortunately for the church-goers of his principality of Moldavia, he won 34 of the 36 battles he waged.

The monasteries can be seen independently or as part of a tour, organised from Suceava or Gura Humorului. Most can be visited from around 9am until darkness falls. Modest dress is expected, which means covered shoulders and long trousers or skirts. Smoking is understandably prohibited, given the age of the wood used in some of the structures.

Vatra Dornei

This former Habsburg spa is now marketing itself as a ski destination, with Ukrainians popping over the border to join the locals on the slopes, mostly suited to beginners. Its other main industry is water-bottling. The water is even said to have curative properties; a sample can be tried at the water fountain in the small castle in Parcul Stațiune. Prior to World War II, Jews maintained a significant presence in the town, represented by a rather run-down synagogue and Jewish cemetery. Its location between various mountain passes makes Vatra Dornei an opportune starting point for hikes into the stunning wilds.

Mănăstirea Voroneț (Voroneț Monastery)

With nearly 50 fine samples from which to choose, picking the top monastery is an impossible task, but Voroneț is certainly a must-see. Its extraordinary frescoes of the Resurrection, the book of Genesis and Judgement Day have earned it the moniker 'the Sistine Chapel of the East'. The intense shade of blue used in the frescoes is now known as 'Voroneț blue'. The place was built by Stephen the Great for Daniel the Hermit, an abbot who had encouraged the prince not to give up on his battle against the Turks.

An eye-catching fresco at Voroneț Monastery

Drive: Suceava monasteries

The idea of going from monastery to monastery may seem like it would induce church fatigue. However, anyone who goes to the effort of reaching Suceava is certainly here for its monastic architecture, and it is therefore worth devoting a day to the task. Dragomirna and Putna are the furthest on this 220-km (140-mile) circuit and can be excluded for a shorter drive.

Start at Suceava. Follow signs for the E85 to Ukraine. After 4km (2¹/₂ miles) turn right to Dragomirna Monastery.

1 Dragomirna
Built at the start of the 17th century, the monastery stands out for its unusual proportions – less than 10m (33ft) wide, and with a 42-m (138-ft) tower. The refectory houses a museum of medieval art, and there is another, smaller church in the grounds.
Head back the way you came. Instead of going into the centre of Suceava, take a right-hand loop round in the direction of Gura Humorului on the E576, drive 25km (15¹/₂ miles) and turn right in the direction of Cacica. After 20km (12¹/₂ miles) and passing through Cacica, you'll arrive at Solca.

2 Solca
Solca lost its iconostasis to Dragomirna when the Austrians closed the monastery in 1785. However, in the 17th century the monks had founded a

brewery which survived and is now one of the oldest in the country.
Continue on the road until it ends. Go left to Putna.

3 Putna
One of Stephen the Great's offerings, the 15th-century Putna faced a four-year wait for consecration because the Moldavians were too busy fighting. It was significantly rebuilt in the 17th century.
Retrace the route, turning right onto the 17A to Sucevița at Marginea. If you reach Solca you've overshot.

4 Sucevița
The largest of the Bucovina monasteries. Painted on the inside and outside, one section of wall remains blank; legend has it that it was because the painter fell off the scaffolding and died, and fellow workers were too superstitious to replace him.
Carry on along the same scenic road, through the Ciumârna Pass. Turn right at Vatra Moldoviței to the monastery.

5 Moldoviţei

Built in the 16th century, Moldoviţei has the look of a fortress. Its marvellous collection of bright frescoes is impressive.

Turn back and follow the road right directly to Gura Humorului. When you reach it, take a left; the monastery is 5km (3 miles) down the road.

6 Humor

Surrounded by ramparts, it has well-preserved frescoes dating back to 1535. It is now a convent.

Drive back to the main road, go right and left soon after. You'll soon reach Voroneţ.

7 Voroneţ

This last monastery will be the highlight of your day (*see p99*).

From Voroneţ, return to the main road and turn right, then follow signs back to Suceava.

The Black Sea coast and Danube Delta

For Romanians, holidays often come down to a straight choice between the mountains and the sea. The coast's ephemeral appeal (few local people would dream of going outside of season) means that summer sees Romanians hit the beach in their droves, giving some resorts a lively, if crowded, atmosphere. To the north, approaching Ukraine, the River Danube meets the shore at the Danube Delta, Europe's largest remaining natural wetland. The result is miles of peaceful waterways, home to an abundant plant and bird life.

To make the most of the Romanian seaside, or *litoral*, it helps to know what to expect. With a couple of exceptions, namely the two largest resorts of Constanţa and Mamaia, facilities at the coastal towns are pretty basic. Accommodation is functional without being luxurious, and the majority of restaurants serve up an uninspiring menu of standard Romanian dishes plus pizza. What you get is a simple, no-frills holiday by the sea. The lack of sophisticated restaurants and upmarket hotels does nothing to dampen the enthusiasm of the local holiday-makers, and the more youth-oriented resorts can have a great atmosphere of fun and freedom. As Romanians find going to the coast in cold weather a little perverse, even if you go slightly out of season, the smaller resorts have a closed-for-business feel. If you love (or loathe)

deserted beaches, time your trip accordingly.

Facilities are fairly similar at the delta. Many Romanians choose to camp, which suits the atmosphere of timelessness that this beautiful natural area enjoys. There are plans to increase the current stock of luxury hotels, but for the moment either a tent or a small pension is the norm. The unfussy, Romanian fare, too, is in keeping with the serene delta area, and a meal overlooking meadows or a tranquil body of water is a simple pleasure.

The resorts covered in this section start far south near the Bulgarian border, with what is probably Romania's countercultural capital, Vama Veche, and are, from south to north: Jupiter, Neptun, Costineşti, Eforie Sud, Eforie Nord, Constanţa and Mamaia. Aside from the northern two, the distances between the towns are generally small. All the Black Sea resorts are clustered within the bottom part of the coastline and the delta is significantly further north.

Constanţa

Constanţa's beaches are usually eschewed in favour of the slightly cleaner ones of the other resorts; it is rather for the culture and history that visitors come to Constanţa, the largest town on the Romanian coast. The port's ancient predecessor was the Greek colony of Tomis, which later became part of the Byzantine Empire. This has left the town with a generous legacy of cultural attractions and as a resort it appeals to anyone who would find non-stop sunbathing boring. It also has a better selection of places to eat than anywhere else on the coast except Mamaia.

The city's main street is Bulevardul Tomis, and although Constanţa itself is

The old casino is one of Constanța's most stylish buildings

one of Romania's largest metropolises, most of what is of interest to the visitor is within walking distance. Fountains around the centre of town are evidence that the authorities are trying to boost the aesthetic appeal of the place, and Constanța has a welcome multicultural feel about it, by dint of a couple of Islamic buildings.

Unfortunately, the glory of many of the buildings is much faded. However, this does not detract from the often lively atmosphere of the main drag and the area around it. The other main walking area is the seafront promenade, where aged accordion players almost give it the feel of old Paris.

Acvariul (Aquarium)
The highlight of Constanța's small aquarium is the middle section, where the big, scary-looking fish are housed.

On the promenade. Tel: (0241) 481 461. www.delfinariu.ro. Open: 9am–8pm. Admission charge.

Catedrala Ortodoxă Sf Petru și Pavel (Orthodox Cathedral of St Peter and St Paul)
Dark and ornate inside, with lots of gold, the neo-Byzantine cathedral was built in 1884. It has much more of the ambience of a place of worship than a tourist attraction, and you may be lucky enough to catch some of a service, which usually involves a priest shaking incense and preaching in a low hum. There is a shop outside, to the right of the entrance, selling icons. By the cathedral, on the side closest to the sea, is an archaeological site with finds from the 4th to 6th centuries.
Strada Arhiepiscopiei 25. Open: 7am–8pm. Free admission.

Moscheea Mare Mahmoud II (Great Mahmudiye Mosque)

Romania's main mosque, built in 1823, has a calm atmosphere, aided by the pleasant plant-filled courtyard outside. Note that the carpeted area is sectioned off. The top of the minaret is accessible, and offers a wonderful panorama of the city and shipyard, but be warned that the narrow, 140-step climb has no handrails.
Strada Crângului 5. Open: 9.30am–9.30pm. Admission charge.

Muzeul de Artă Populară (Museum of Popular Art)

This is an enjoyable museum with icons, traditional costumes, old photographs and archaeological finds.

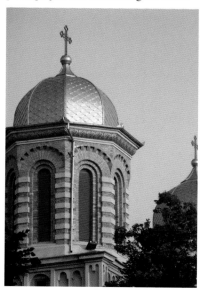

The Catedrala Ortodoxă is a distinctive point on the town's skyline

MARIA TĂNASE

High-school dropout Maria Tănase (1913–63) was little known until the age of 25. By then a member of a theatrical troupe, she recorded some folk songs, the first recordings for Romanian Radio. Two years later they were destroyed by the fascist Iron Guard, on the pretext that they 'distorted local folklore' – although the singer's friendships with Jewish intellectuals are thought to have been the real motivation. Tănase continued her rise to prominence, singing for soldiers wounded in World War II and at the Christmas festivities at the Royal Cavalry Regiment, attended by members of the monarchy and government. In the 1950s she was awarded the State Prize and title of Artist Emerita.

Two temporary exhibition rooms are given over to a new display every two months. Some items are accompanied by captions in English and the staff will do their best to explain things. The museum is housed in a lovely two-level building, whose previous incarnations were as city hall and post office. A well-stocked gift shop sells jewellery, bags, traditional clothes and a wealth of other Romanian crafts.
Bulevardul Tomis 32. Tel: (0241) 616 133. www.muzeuetno.lx.ro. Open: 9am–8pm (summer); 9am–5pm (winter). Admission charge.

Muzeul de Istorie Națională și Arheologie (Archaeological and Historical Museum)

Highlights of this large museum include mammoths' tusks, the bones of an ancient woman, and the Glykon serpent, carved from a single piece of marble, a striking combination of lion, snake, antelope and human body parts. More recent history is also touched upon.

Piaţa Ovidiu 12. Tel: (0241) 618 763. Open: Mon–Sun 8am–8pm (May–Sept); Wed–Sun 9am–5pm (Oct–Apr). Admission charge.

Parcul Arheologic (Archaeological Park)

This large, pretty park showcases ruins of Tomis that date back as far as the 3rd and 4th centuries, the most impressive (and identifiable) of which are some tall columns and large urns. Quite ornate detail is visible on some of the exhibits. Unfortunately, though, there's nothing by way of explanation,

A picturesque sunset at the Danube Delta

THE PETROL STATION-FREE SUNSHINE HIGHWAY

Drivers might notice something odd about the partially finished A2, the so-called Sunshine Highway (Autostrada Soarelui) which goes from Bucharest to Constanţa; there's a complete lack of petrol stations. There are in fact some stations in the vicinity of the road, down the roads leading off from the main highway, but as a driver new to the area you would not know it. For the time being, it's better to have a full tank before you set off, rather than venture into an unknown backwater in the hope of finding somewhere to fill up. The large petrol firms are planning several petrol stations for the highway itself during 2008.

and most locals simply use the venue as a park.

Corner of Bulevardul Ferdinand & Bulevardul Tomis. Free admission.

Costineşti

Costineşti is not the next resort up after Vama Veche, but Romanians tend to think of the two as a pair, as both cater to the youth market. But whereas in Vama Veche the music of choice is rock and indie, here you're more likely to hear *manele* (kitsch pop inspired by Balkan love songs) emanating from the bars.

Little of the atmosphere remains of the fishing village from 50 years ago. The beach is approached by a road lined with stalls selling fried fish, doughnuts, kebabs (this is not a resort for health freaks), inflatables, flip-flops and other seaside paraphernalia.

Aiming at the youth demographic, Costineşti has quite a few water-sports options, including banana boating, windsurfing, jetskiing and canoeing, some of which can be pursued on the lake set a little way back from the beach. The beach itself is a little stony, and is traversed by young men playing tinny recorded adverts for local water-sports operators. A rusty old shipwreck at the northern end, the Greek vessel *Evangelia*, which has been there since the 1960s, provides a focal point. Despite not having a particularly cultural atmosphere, the town plays host to a film festival in August; features are shown with English subtitles.

Danube Delta

The delta is Europe's youngest and least stable landscape. Its dynamism is a result of the alluvium deposited by the River Danube, which increases its width by about 40m (over 130ft) every year. It consists of three main branches, or 'arms', Chilia, Sulina and Sfântu Gheorghe, which derive their names from the ports where they meet the sea. Between them are a multitude of channels, carving up the territory into reed, marsh, island and forest areas. The rise and fall of the water levels, which flood much of the area in spring and autumn, continually reshape and redefine the terrain.

Romania shares the delta with Ukraine, causing some political tension of late. Its surface area is variously estimated at between 2,500 and about 5,000sq km (965 and 1,930sq miles), with about four fifths in Romanian territory. The total population of the delta for the two countries combined is 15,000. Traditionally, the inhabitants earned their living by catching the 45 freshwater species of fish that frequent the area, but today an increasing number

Roman remains like the ruins of Halmyris in the Danube Delta are another highlight

Some 300 species of birds visit the delta, making it a twitcher's paradise

of people have joined the tourist industry. Visitors come not only for the wildlife (although the 300 bird species make the delta a twitcher's paradise), but also for the wonderful and diverse views and sheer tranquillity.

It is impossible to single out particular places in the delta as more worthy of attention than any other, although busier arteries tend to have fewer birds and fish, which are deterred by the presence of too many humans. Therefore you're likely to get more out of spending a full day sailing deep into the delta than if you just go out on a boat for a couple of hours. However, even the shortest trip will yield plenty and still convey the glory and uniqueness of the delta.

Sfântu Gheorghe

Sfântu Gheorghe is just above the southeast 'corner' of the delta. The caviar capital, this is where the sturgeon that produce the black delicacy are caught. It is also the rather unlikely setting for an August film festival. A fishing village, Sfântu Gheorghe is sleepy, and the empty beaches make a striking change from the Black Sea coast in high season. The only 'sight' is an ugly Communist windmill, now as obsolete as the regime that built it.

Sulina

Former shipping town Sulina, the delta's third main hub, does have the air of a place that has seen better days. The easternmost point of Romania, its cemetery, 19th-century waterfront houses and lighthouse bear testimony to its heritage. It also has a decent stretch of sand, and nascent seaside tourism is taking root here.

Tulcea

Most people travelling to the delta will pass through Tulcea, a hub for tour operators organising delta sorties. The town is also worth half a day's visit. Its wide riverfront promenade, where a phalanx of boats is moored, is pleasant for a stroll and frequented by amorous couples as well as eager delta-tour touts. Tulcea spent nearly half a millennium under Ottoman control, and its mosque, catering to the Turkish contingent, gives it a slightly different feel from a typically homogeneous Romanian town, although it does have the usual quota of churches, art museums and so on.

Eforie Nord

One of the largest resorts of the southern cluster, Eforie Nord is also home to a yacht club, which gives it a more upmarket air than many of its neighbours. More sedate, too, it lacks the loud music of the more youth-oriented resorts. This is predominantly a family place, with swings, volleyball

and football pitches on the beach. Unlike elsewhere on the coast, thought has gone into the facilities here, even to the extent of yellow beach cubicles where swimmers can change. The people are a far cry from the brash young topless crowd further south. The restaurants, too, are generally more civilised.

Away from the beach, there's a park featuring several statues and benches on which to sit and study them. The resort is also popular with health tourists (*see pp118–19*).

Eforie Sud

Eforie Sud is a lot more quiet and relaxed than its northern counterpart. Unlike most of the other beaches, there is no blaring music, and there are fewer tourists and less infrastructure. Even the beach itself, sandy and pleasant, enjoys some seclusion from the town. Benches dotted along the clifftop are nice spots to sit and enjoy the view without getting sandy.

Jupiter

While not as youth-oriented as Vama Veche and Costineşti, Jupiter is also relatively popular with younger holiday-makers, partly due to its large campsite and decent, fine-sand beach. A forest and artificial lake confer a certain prettiness on Jupiter. The Communist hotels are striking if you like that kind of thing. There's also a tourist train that wends its way around the place.

Boat trip: Danube Delta

There really is no end of different boat trips that can be taken in the delta, from quick jaunts of a couple of hours to forays lasting days, and with the ever-changing landscape these vary from month to month. If the weather is warm, sun cream and mosquito repellent will be vital for a comfortable journey.

Allow one full day for this 120-km (75-mile) trip.

Note that the slow ferry goes at most once a day, so if you want to hop off you will have to find alternative transport or re-board 24 hours later.

Start in Tulcea. Either take the bumpy delta road DJ222C or sail for 12km (7 miles) to Nufăru.

1 Nufăru

Previously the Roman town of Talamonium, Nufăru, which was destroyed and re-built, has yielded up archaeological discoveries from the 12th and 13th centuries, including Roman and Byzantine coins.

By boat, continue to Bălteni de Jos, the ferry's first port of call.

2 Bălteni de Jos

The scene of a fortified settlement as early as the Iron Age, the village of Bălteni de Jos (Upper Bălteni) is now the preserve of fishermen and a small number of pensions for the tourist trade.

Continue to the next ferry stop, Mahmudia, which is also on the road from Tulcea.

3 Mahmudia

The rather run-down town of Mahmudia, 35km (22 miles) southeast of Tulcea, occupies the site of the Salsovia stronghold. The Roman-Byzantine fortress, the remains of which are still visible, is thought to be the place where the Roman Emperor Falvius Licinius is said to have met his premature end at the behest of Constantine the Great, who suspected him of attempting to raise troops among the Barbarians.

Continue by road or boat to Murighiol, which is also an occasional ferry stop.

4 Murighiol

Seeing sleepy Murighiol, it's hard to believe that in past times it was of vital strategic importance. The Roman town Halmyris once stood at this point where the Danube reached the Black Sea, thereby offering a gateway to the Middle East. Roman Emperor Trajan fought two wars and built a plethora of forts to wrest it from the Dacians and secure Roman control of the delta. The site is also home to the tomb of two Christian martyrs, Epictet and Astion. Slightly set back from the village, visitors can explore the ruins of the Roman town.

From here, hire a local boat for the trip to Uzlina.

5 Uzlina

The fishing village and lake of the same name can be visited in a short boat trip. The lakes here give rise to an especially rich bird life, including a protected pelican colony, quite thrilling to behold. The Danube Delta Biosphere Reserve (*see p123*) and an EcoInfoCentre are also based in the village.

The rest of the journey is by water only. Back in Murighiol, board the ferry or boat and continue along the channel to the port of Sfântu Gheorghe.

6 Sfântu Gheorghe

(*See pp108–9.*)
Take a boat back to Tulcea.

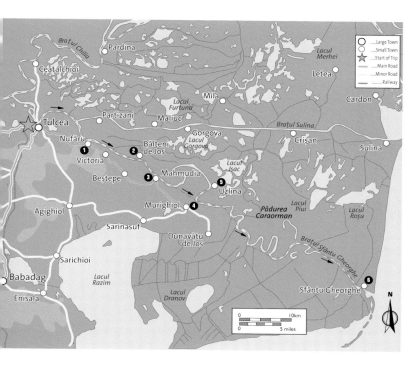

Watersports are a growing seaside industry

Apart from its size, Mamaia stands out for the quality and variety of its services. All sorts of different cuisines are available, and many of the restaurants and clubs are outlets of professionally run Bucharest chains, which is why many foreigners choose Mamaia as their holiday destination.

Another group that is particularly well catered for in Mamaia is children. A raft of things to do, from mini-boating lakes and a large aqua park to bouncy castles and reverse bungee, plus all manner of wandering clowns, performance artists and balloon sellers, will keep even the most demanding youngsters entertained. The beach slopes gently and the sea is generally safe for swimming.

Aqua Magic

Watery fun with tube slides, rubber rings and lots of sunbeds for parents. *Opposite Hotel Perla. Tel: (0241) 831 183. Open: 8am–10pm (mid-May–mid-Sept). Admission charge.*

Mamaia

The closest thing Romania has to a proper, bustling seaside resort, big Mamaia (8km/5 miles long) consists of a long, broad walkway, just behind the wide beach, with hotels mostly set along small, perpendicular roads going off it. The walkway hosts almost every service you might need; restaurants, bars, clubs, clothes shops, small supermarkets and children's entertainment.

Telegondola (cable car)

Mamaia's cable car takes passengers on a 2-km (1¼-mile) ride along the seafront and back. It's useful transport, but more people use it as a fun way to enjoy the fine views. Board at either the Perla complex at the southern end or near the casino in the north. *Open: 10am–11pm. Admission charge, except for children, and for passengers with disabilities and their accompaniers.*

Neptun

Leafy Neptun bears much similarity to the efficient and purpose-built Black Sea resorts down in Bulgaria. What is lacking in naturalness is certainly made up for in convenience and standards, however, as there are shopping centres, eateries, entertainment venues and sports facilities aplenty. The former location of Ceauşescu's villa and private beach, and the modern-day resort of choice for the president, Neptun has retained a certain air of exclusivity. The clientele is mainly comprised of wealthy, older locals and a few foreigners, and the hotels and restaurants are among the best on the coast outside Constanţa and Mamaia. The resort's reliability also means it is frequented by package tours.

The beach, which boasts an international blue flag licence, has been arranged tastefully, with wooden beach umbrellas and walkways. Loud house music is pumped out for sunbathers. A stone jetty extends out to sea, from the end of which you can sometimes take a boat trip, provided the marine conditions allow. As well as the rows of sunbeds, a couple of four-poster beds with curtains are available to rent. There are two large artificial lakes where you can get some peace and quiet. A small tourist train ferries visitors around the resort. Neptun does have some nightlife, although the kind of visitors who pitch up here are unlikely to cite partying as a priority.

The Black Sea coast and Danube Delta

Eforie Nord, one of the coast's more upscale options

The Roma

Little is known of the origins of the
Roma (or gypsies, Roma or Romanies,
as they are variously termed), largely
due to their lack of a written history.
It is generally thought that they came
from India's Punjab and Rajastan
regions, migrating to Europe and North
Africa from the middle of the 11th
century to escape their positions at the
bottom of a rigid caste hierarchy.
Linguistic and genetic evidence
supports this theory. Both physically
and in dress, the Roma bear a close
resemblance to Indians of those areas.

Romania's Roma population is
officially estimated at over half a
million, or 2.5 per cent of the country's
total. This on its own would make
them a significant minority. But the
failure of some Roma families to
register newborn babies and apply for
proper documentation has led certain
commentators to conclude that the
real figure could be up to four times
as high.

There is significant division between
the Roma and ethnic Romanians. The
latter attribute their country's poor
reputation in Europe to Roma who
leave the country to beg and steal.
Ţigani, or gypsies, are also considered
responsible for a disproportionate
amount of crime in their homeland.

Public perceptions of the Roma
community sank even further in 2003,
when the 12-year-old daughter of the
so-called King of the Roma was made
to marry a 15-year-old boy, despite
fleeing the unofficial and illegal
ceremony. The marriage and
subsequent consummation were
widely condemned.

Roma advocates counter that
outsiders do not properly understand
the community traditions and way of
life, and that the high level of
discrimination against the group
marginalises and excludes them from
the legitimate labour market. But not
all Roma live in poverty. Some clans,
like the Kalderash, for example,
prospered through their traditional
coppersmith work. Large mansions
with distinctive tin roofs can
sometimes be found in otherwise
deprived Roma districts.

As an officially categorised minority,
the Roma are assured representation in
parliament, and where they constitute
at least a fifth of the population, their
language, the Indo-Aryan language
Romani, also receives official
recognition. Several programmes and
associations also fight for their rights
and inclusion, including the National
Agency for the Roma.

Whatever the state of relations, Roma culture has had a huge influence on mainstream Romanian society. Wedding singers and musicians, or *lăutari*, are often of Roma origin, and tourists seek out traditional Roma villages that have a strong musical tradition. *Manele*, kitschy pop music descended from Balkan love songs, is also a Roma genre, influenced by traditional Roma music and predominantly performed by singers drawn from the community.

Romania is also home to the first declared 'Roma state'. Iulian Rădulescu had previously declared himself the emperor of the world's Roma. In 1997 he announced at a press conference that due to a decree he had signed, a deprived district in Târgu Jiu, in the southwest of the country, was henceforth Cem Romengo, the state of the Romanies. A symbolic entity, it was to have no borders, no army, and did not affect Romanian sovereignty, said Rădulescu.

A traditional upscale Roma house

Vama Veche

Eastern Europe's answer to Goa, Vama Veche has a reputation for counterculture. Hippies, rockers and other young rebels are drawn by its laidback feel. A plan to replace its dirt tracks with proper roads was vigorously opposed. In fact, feelings

TRAIAN BĂSESCU

One of Romania's most colourful politicians, Traian Băsescu started his career as a merchant marine officer and was promoted to ship's captain. After 1989, he joined the group that emerged to take power in the immediate aftermath of the revolution, and in 1991 became minister of transport. He was eventually elected leader of the Democratic Party, and then mayor of Bucharest, in which capacity he was credited with reducing the city's stray dog population, earning a visit from a concerned Brigitte Bardot. After re-election, Băsescu quit as mayor to run – successfully – for president. Despite some un-PC gaffes, he remains popular, and easily defeated his opponents' attempts to impeach him in a 2007 public referendum.

There is no shortage of paraphernalia on sale in seaside resorts

run so high about preserving the special character of the resort that it had its own association, devoted to the purpose, called Save Vama Veche. It may not be quite the haven of non-conformism it thinks it is: Communist uniformity is still too deeply entrenched in people's mentality for that, but people still camp out on the beach and the police turn a blind eye to the odd instance of nudism (which generally occurs after a high amount of alcohol has been consumed).

There are a few reminders (such as the beach stall selling books) that the resort was in Communist times reserved exclusively for the staff of the university at Cluj, and its character developed out of these intellectual beginnings. The village consists of the

Vama Veche is the resort of choice for the country's hippie and alternative community

beach and a few small roads surrounding it, and it is quite impossible to get lost.

The nightlife is the major point of Vama Veche (which means 'Old Customs Point' – the town is within walking distance of the Bulgarian border). Music blasts out on the beach all night, free-standing kiosks sell beer in plastic cups and several venues stage live music. The up-for-it studenty crowd creates a vibe that makes this one of the most distinctive resorts on the coast.

Health tourism

Romanians' love of beer and sausages may not mark the country out as the most health-obsessed of states. But the Roman and Habsburg occupations left the place with a tradition of visiting spas, which has burgeoned into a current total of 160 spa resorts. Add to that one third of Europe's mineral springs (3,000 in total), the low prices of medical treatment and increasingly easier access from Western Europe, and you get a huge potential for health tourism, which is now beginning to attract visitors from abroad.

Local spa resorts and treatment centres take quite a forensic attitude to their work. The various health resorts make specific promises of what ailments they can treat. A comprehensive list is impossible but the following should convey the breadth of afflictions for which spas offer hope of improvement: Băile Herculane (eye and stomach disorders, rheumatism); Sovata (gynaecological disorders); Călimăneşti (gastritis, ulcers, liver and gall bladder problems, stiff joints, neurological, gyneacological and cardiovascular complaints); Ocna Sibiului (rheumatic, dermatological, allergenic, metabolic and gynaecological issues); and Borsec (nutritional and metabolic illnesses).

Spa managers are similarly precise and scientific about the various curative elements. Black Sea water is described as 'chlorided, sulphated, sodic and magnesian', mineral waters as 'sulphurous, chlorided, bicarbonated, sodic, calcic and mezothermal'. Mud baths (warm and cold), the breathing in of volcanic

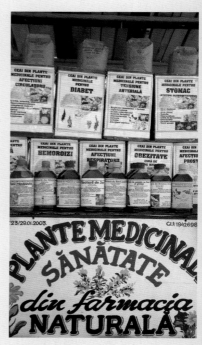

Romanians place great store in natural remedies

Sunflower seeds are without doubt the country's favourite health food

fumes and the drinking of special waters are combined with various complementary therapies to offer guests the full health package. Some people spend upwards of two weeks on an intensive package, and return repeatedly.

Many health resorts can be found by the sea. Eforie Nord, whose spa has been operating for over a century, Neptun and Mangalia are the three big names on the Black Sea coast. The other main area for spas is the mountains, where spring waters and bracing air – said to have the perfect balance of ozone and ions – are recommended for a host of nervous complaints. Some spas date back as far as Roman times. The word *băile* in a town's name indicates that it is home to a spa.

Romanian spas are said to have had some famous devotees. Băile Herculane, in the west of the country, is so called because of the legend that Hercules himself stopped there to bathe in the natural spring waters. And Emperor Napoleon III of France is said to have drunk the waters of Călimăneşti, in southern Romania, in preference to those of his homeland.

In recent years, a new kind of health tourism has sprung up. With long waiting lists for state-funded treatment and the high costs of private care in some Western European countries, patients are heading eastwards in search of cheaper, quicker procedures. The areas being marketed by Romanian clinics include dentistry and plastic surgery. Two proponents of the latter are the pop group The Cheeky Girls, who left their adopted homeland of Britain to return to their native Romania for breast enlargement surgery – although they did have to make a return trip to have the procedure corrected.

Getting away from it all

Remote regions, untouched by Communism and Capitalism alike, showcase a Romania preserved in time, where the landscape has stood still for centuries, and where the frantic growth of Bucharest and its big, bland apartment blocks seem as though they belong to a different country. Tiny hamlets, mountain sorties and the country's national parks all provide opportunities to marvel at the great wildernesses of this Eastern European state.

If you want to see any of the more peaceful, remote areas, it really helps to have your own transport. That is not to say that none of them can be reached with public transport and legwork – some can. But the various train, bus, maxi-taxi and cab combinations required will demand a lot of time, patience, planning and a good sense of humour. The furthest outposts are simply not accessible via public transport, and in these cases, the non-driver's best option is to negotiate and hire a taxi for the whole day.

Homestays

One of the best ways to experience rural Romania is with a village homestay. The practice of renting out a spare room or two is a common one in all the places of interest to tourists, even in larger cities like Braşov. But homestays really come into their own in rural areas that are still largely ignored by big hotels. In such environments, it is often just a case of looking for signs in windows or outside homes that say *cazare* (accommodation).

It is important to consider what you want out of the homestay. Some take the form of rustic hotels, with several rooms with television, a restaurant and

Homestays are a wonderful way to get to know the real Romania

Getting away from it all

other mod cons. Others are much more basic, with fairly primitive washing facilities. If you're taking the official route, the place will be graded using a set number of daisies, a similar idea to the hotel star system. Accommodation ranked with four or five daisies will offer large bedrooms with private wash facilities. Such places are in the minority. At one or two daisies, the rooms may be on the poky side, and you'll share a bathroom with the other guests and sometimes the owners and their family.

Many homestays are unregistered. This does not indicate that the owners are disreputable; it's just a common way of avoiding the reams of bureaucracy and high charges involved in officially registering a business of this kind in Romania. In such cases, you can simply ask to see the facilities before committing.

Rural areas offer a real escape from the bustle of everyday life

Also have a think about how much privacy or interaction you are after. In some cases, families are keen only to make some money from a spare room. They do not provide any food, and will leave you to your own devices – ideal if you value your own space and independence. But other travellers see the homestay as a means of getting acquainted with ordinary Romanians, and learning a bit more about their culture, customs and way of life. Some homestays will give you the opportunity for this kind of contact. The proprietor will provide meals, and may even organise some activities or show you around the local area. The following organisations are useful resources:

ANTREC, or Asociaţia Naţională de Turism Rural şi Ecologic (National Association of Rural, Ecological and Cultural Tourism). Bulevardul Marasti 59, Sector 1, Bucharest. Tel: (021) 222 8001. www.antrec.ro

European Centre for Eco-Agro Tourism (ECEAT). c/o Focus Eco Centre. Tel: (0265) 163 692. www.eceat.org

Opération Villages Roumains. c/o Pan Travel. Strada Grozăvescu, Cluj. Tel: (0264) 420 516. Email: mail@pantravel.ro

The mountains of Bucegi have been designated a Nature Reserve

National parks

While the lack of human incursion into areas of wilderness has helped them remain unspoiled, the downside is that few of Romania's national parks have much in the way of facilities for visitors. This can make finding your way around them unaided rather difficult. Some, but not all, are accessible by public transport. In total, the country has upwards of 500 protected areas, of which a dozen have been classified as national parks, and one, the Danube Delta, a World Heritage Site.

Apart from those listed below, other national parks, and their counties, are: Călimani (Bistriţa-Năsăud, Harghita, Mureş, Suceava), Ceahlău (Neamţ), Cheile Bicazului-Hăşmaş (Harghita, Neamţ), Cheile Nerei-Beuşniţa (Caraş-Severin), Cozia (Vâlcea), Domogled-Valea Cernei (Caraş-Severin, Gorj, Mehedinţi), Piatra Craiului (Argeş, Braşov), Rodna (Bistriţa-Năsăud,

Maramureş, Suceava), Semenic-Cheile Caraşului (Caraş Severin).

Parcul Naţional Munţii Măcinului (Măcin Mountains National Park)

Close to the Danube in Tulcea County, the predominantly granite mountain range is the oldest in the country and among the oldest in Europe, having formed in the Paleozoic period. Temperature changes have resulted in erosion, which gives the slopes the aspect of ruins. Various threatened forms of fauna have made their home in the mountains. Lakes, peaks and Romanian fortresses are among the highlights.

Tulcea. Tel: (0240) 515 505.
www.muntiimacin.ro/eu

Parcul Naţional Retezat (Retezat National Park)

Part of the southern Carpathians, the country's oldest national park was established in 1935. It boasts the highest

number of mountain peaks over 2,000m (6,560ft) in the country, a total of more than 20, plus the deepest glacial lake, of which it has more than 80. It has now been designated a UNESCO Biosphere Reserve, and has expanded to four times its initial range. Black mountain goats, bears and stags are among the creatures that inhabit the area.
www.retezat.ro

Parcul Naţional Porţile de Fier (Iron Gates National Park)

Straddling Romania and Serbia, this huge park, totalling 115,655sq km (44,650sq miles), covers the area where the Danube first enters Romanian territory. Some hold it to be the most spectacular stretch of the river. Dramatic gorges and stunning river views eerily reflecting the peaks that rise up above them are among the reasons why.

Str. Banatului 92, Orşova. Tel: (0252) 362 596. www.portiledefierpn.ro

Rezervaţia Biosferei Delta Dunării (Danube Delta Biosphere Reserve)

The only one of Romania's national parks that has proper visitor facilities is also a UNESCO protected site (*see pp107–9*). Many tourists choose to start their delta sortie from Tulcea, which has a decent array of hotels and is the main town here.
34A Portului, Tulcea. Tel: (0240) 518 945. www.ddbra.ro

Rezervaţia Floristică Todirescu (Todirescu Flower Reservation)

Over a century old, the reservation is part of the Rarău Massif in southern Bucovina. In July it is home to a dazzling display of flowers, including chrysanthemums, daffodils, bluebells and daisies.

Dramatic scenery on the way to the Bicaz Gorges

Getting away from it all

Rezervația Naturală Bucegi (Bucegi Nature Reserve)

The nature reserve covers the entirety of the mountain range of the same name in Prahova Valley. Not only is it rich in fauna, but it has also preserved the traditional way of life, and you may come upon shepherds and their flocks and other such pastoral scenes. Plans to develop a ski run in the area have concerned environmentalists.

Behind the Hotel Palace, Bucegi. Tel: (0244) 311 750. www.apmph.ro. Open: Tue–Sun 9am–7pm, Mon 9am–5pm.

Mountain areas

Without doubt, Romania's mountains are one of its chief assets. The Carpathians (alternatively known as the Transylvanian Alps), which make up about a third of the country's territory, are home to some of the most stunning scenery in the land, with imposing peaks rising up majestically and dense forests that hide bold bears and furtive wolves. Mountainous areas are certainly not the easiest parts of Romania in which to travel, but they are among the most rewarding.

Despite never having visited them, Irish novelist Bram Stoker extolled the Carpathians, 'one of the wildest and least known portions of Europe' in *Dracula*. Describing them as 'full of beauty of every kind', he wrote of 'a green sloping land full of forests and woods', 'little towns or castles on the

Fir-covered mountains are a typically Romanian scene

top of steep hills such as we see in old missals', 'mighty slopes of forest up to the lofty steeps of the Carpathians themselves' and 'an endless perspective of jagged rock and pointed crags, till these were themselves lost in the distance, where the snowy peaks rose grandly'.

Impressive though Stoker's research was, it is even more remarkable that much of what he wrote remains just as accurate today. So long free from human incursion, the remote parts of the mountains retain their isolated, Middle Ages feel, and as such are a great place to get away from it all and enjoy an untouched, serene and magnificent part of Europe.

While drivers can make significant inroads into elevated territory on the many winding (though often bumpy) mountainside roads, to get the best out of the mountains it is better to hike and cycle. This is done with the aid of coloured markers delineating routes, a decent map and a network of mountain cabanas providing respite and shelter, some of which are more luxurious than others. A third and less conventional option is the horse. Specialist holiday firms organise horseback treks through mountainous areas stopping off at villages, allowing you access to some of the furthest-flung places.

As well as outstanding mountain scenery, including gorges, passes, massifs, glacial lakes, forests thick with fir trees, snow-capped peaks, rivers and

The Făgăraş mountains rise imposingly in the distance

rainbows, the Carpathians are the last great European refuge of several large carnivores, as well as other creatures (*see pp72–3*). The time-honoured ways of life, long forgotten by most of Western Europe, are another joy of mountain journeys. They are also now under threat, due both to members of remote communities emigrating to other European Union countries for higher wages, and to EU health and safety regulations that conflict with the traditional methods of dairy farming still in use in the villages.

Before setting off, it's vital to be well prepared. The weather can be subject to sudden changes, and a clement day at the foot of the mountain does not automatically mean decent weather further up. Take advice from local groups about routes and conditions (the network of cabanas is a good source for this).

When to go

The year in Romania divides roughly into four seasons that correspond to the weather in the rest of mainland Europe and the UK. Changes from one season to another can take place quite abruptly. Summer and winter, both of which can bring extremes of temperature, seem to be getting longer of late, and many Romanians bemoan the gradual loss of the four distinct and relatively reliable seasons, which they put down to pollution and climate change.

It is true that the hot weather can begin early, sometimes as soon as April, and continue until as late as September. Summer temperatures can be extremely high, and the country has been afflicted by the heatwaves that have struck much of southern Europe in recent years, with temperatures exceeding 40°C (104°F). Bucharest sees a daily average of around 30°C (86°F) throughout the summer months, although it is usually cooler outside the capital, particularly in the mountainous areas. Winters can also be exceedingly chilly, with temperatures plunging to –10°C (14°F) or below. December, January and February are usually the coldest months. Some protection is afforded by the Carpathian mountain range, which acts as a buffer to Atlantic air masses and Russian climatic influences. Spring and autumn can be very agreeable, with long stretches of uninterrupted warm weather. Romania does not have many rainy days (outside its mountain areas), but when it comes the rain often does so with force and accompanied by strong winds and sometimes storms.

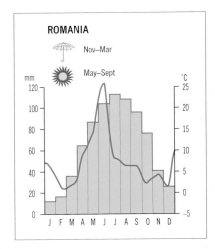

WEATHER CONVERSION CHART

25.4mm = 1 inch

°F = 1.8 × °C + 32

Unless you are particularly fond of extremes of temperature, or have come solely for the ski slopes or the beach, spring and autumn are probably the most pleasant times to schedule a trip. If you're skiing, you can be fairly certain of snow from December to February, but it would be unadvisable to plan a trip much earlier or later if that's the only reason you're coming. Romanians flock to the seaside in July and August, so you may wish to rule those months in or out depending on whether you prioritise a party atmosphere or space on the beach. Summer weekends in Bucharest can be peaceful, as the party set decamps to the beach. Few local people would even entertain the idea of going to the coast during the winter so if you want to walk along deserted (albeit chilly) beaches, that is the ideal time. In colder weather, the mountains are the more popular destinations, and some Romanians spend Christmas there. The best time to visit the Danube Delta is between April and October, with bird migration at its apex in spring and the end of autumn.

The cost of flights to Romania can vary quite significantly, with the peak travelling times of summer (when local people head off on holiday) and Christmas (which sees an exodus of expats) most expensive.

The country has some regional variation. The south is a little warmer than the north, and the southeast enjoys Mediterranean influences. Elevated areas are usually colder than lower lying places, and the cities can be hotter than the countryside (again, many Romanians blame the pollution).

Summer temperatures make a trip to the coast a must

Getting around

Romanian transport has improved significantly from its woeful state under Communism and immediately afterwards, when pot-holed roads, creaking old trains and taxi drivers who could be almost guaranteed to fleece a foreign passenger were the norm. That said, the transport network is not yet up to the standards of Western Europe. But travellers are often willing to put up with the inconveniences and irritations, thanks to the bargain prices.

By air

Domestic flights remain largely the preserve of business travellers; most tourists prefer to take a more scenic option, usually the train, and most Romanians opt for cheaper land transport. The main cities are all served by an airport, and if you want to cover a large distance quickly, an internal flight can be an option, although they are often rather costly. Plane tickets should be booked a few days in advance from a travel agent or online.

By train

Trains are an excellent way to see the Romanian countryside and way of life, but pick your service carefully. There are four kinds of long-distance journeys: *personal, acelerat, rapid* and inter-city. *Personal* trains are the slowest and cheapest. Popular with pensioners and peasants taking their wares to the city to sell, they stop at the unlikeliest of remote hamlets. Great for a flavour of Romanian life, as you will often end up in conversation (regardless of whether your

TREN	NR.	DESTINAȚIA	VIA	ORA	ÎNT.	LINIA
P	9 1 0 3	PIETROSITA	Titu	14:13		2
P	7 0 3 3	URZICENI		14:20		8
A	1 7 2 5	TARGU JIU	Videle	14:45		1
IC	5 5 7	BICAZ	Ploiesti Sud	15:00		8
R	8 2 7	SIBIU	Ploiesti Vest	15:30		7

PLECĂRI-*DEPARTURES*

Romanian trains go all over the country as well as to foreign destinations

The comprehensive Bucharest bus network, although it can be crowded, offers good value for money

interlocutors know English), they can be immensely frustrating if you're in a rush. Inter-city trains are speedy, modern and more expensive, but still good value. First-class accommodation can be plush and such journeys a pleasure. On overnight trains, sleeper compartments are available. Tickets can be bought from the station, usually from a specific window indicated by a sign, or from the CFR (railway) office in town. They may consist of the ticket itself and a separate reservation. Some Romanians commonly fare dodge, paying the conductor a bribe when necessary, although this would be a risky strategy for foreigners.

By car

Thanks in large part to European Union money, Romania's roads are a lot better than they used to be, with some main highways now comparable to Western ones. However, some inter-city routes are still on the bumpy side. A lack of central reservations combined with widespread poor driving and old brakes make fatal accidents more common than in Western Europe. Horses and carts, though rarer than they once were, are another road hazard. On the other hand, car travel is of course convenient and protects you from the vagaries and occasional unpleasantness of public transport.

Like the rest of continental Europe, Romanians drive on the right. Speed limits are 50km/h (31mph) in built-up areas, 90km/h (56mph) on the open road and 130km/h (80mph) on the highway but lower for motorcycles, vans and new drivers. On the highway, oncoming drivers will flash their lights to warn you of police up ahead, upon which everyone slows dramatically and drives past the police at an almost

The station concourse at the Gara de Nord has been renovated since Communist times

surreally slow pace. If you get a ticket, you must pay it (at a discount if you do so within a few days) at any post office. Front seatbelts are compulsory, but not back. You're not allowed to talk on your phone while driving but everybody does. Parking is tricky in the cities, and although illegal parking abounds, if you want to avoid a possible (though improbable) fine, pay car parks are your best bet.

Car rental is more expensive than in more developed countries, but major cities all have several outlets. You need to take your passport and driving licence and leave a deposit.

By local public transport
Bus, trolleybus and tram
In most cities and smaller towns, the cheapest way of getting around is by a combination of bus, trolleybus and tram. The vehicles may seem somewhat rickety – except in the larger cities where the fleets are being upgraded – and in smaller locales stops may lack obvious indication, but the service is usually reliable and fairly comprehensive. The usual procedure is to buy a ticket from a booth by the stop and validate it using the on-board machine. If you're staying a while, a monthly or multi-journey pass (also available from booths or station ticket offices) can be a good investment. If found without a ticket you will be fined; at such times when the booth is closed (after 9pm in the capital and from 2pm on Sunday) you're unlikely to encounter an inspector. All forms of transport can get horrendously busy at peak times, and you should always take

care to protect your valuables from pickpockets.

Few tourists opt for the bus service, which is less comfortable and comprehensive than the train. More useful is the maxi-taxi, a minibus that's open to the public. It can be difficult to find the departure point, and journeys are often cramped, but maxi-taxis are convenient if your destination is not reachable by train. Buy your ticket from the driver.

Metro

While not as comprehensive as the bus and tram network, the underground system in Bucharest, called the Metro, is cheaper, usually less crowded than the above-ground public transport, and is a good option if you're travelling right across the city. Tickets are on sale from offices and kiosks at the stations and must be inserted into a turnstile when you enter the system. Newer trains, replacing the old graffiti-covered ones, are patrolled by slightly menacing guards. There are few route maps displayed throughout the system, so it's advisable to have some idea of where you're going before you set off.

By taxi

While prices have soared in recent years, taxis are still a relatively cheap way to get around in Romania. They can either be booked by phone or hailed on the street; the former is slightly safer for foreigners as it eliminates the chance of getting a rogue driver with a dodgy meter who will charge an unwitting foreigner several times the proper fare or at the least take a circuitous route. If you do pick one up in the street, make sure the price per kilometre is displayed on the vehicle and ask the driver to activate the meter if he does not do so automatically. Avoid any taxi with the number 9403 on the side; it's a dishonest independent driver trying to make his car seem part of a legitimate cab firm.

Tram is another convenient way to get around in Bucharest

Accommodation

Accommodation options have not quite kept pace with Romania's general economic progress since the fall of Communism, and hotels in the country can often be overpriced, substandard or both. Five-star hotels with international standards and prices to match but also cheaper facilities, including campsites and youth hostels, can be found. For a more authentic view of Romania, homestays can provide an insight into the local culture.

Standards vary widely, with neither price nor star ranking serving as an accurate guide. Unless you're paying top whack in an established brand hotel, service is likely to be largely indifferent, particularly in the south and along the coast. While in many areas it is fairly safe to turn up and be sure of getting a bed for the night, there are times when it makes sense to book in advance. Accommodation at the delta can fill up in high season, as can city youth hostels, and the coast is besieged by weekenders from Bucharest throughout July and August.

In most accommodation, little attention has been paid to the needs of guests with disabilities. Steps, uneven flooring, the absence of lifts and poky bathrooms are just a few of the obstacles that anyone with limited mobility will face. The only sure way of circumventing them is to stay at the more expensive hotels, which have lifts, rooms fitted out for guests with disabilities and obliging staff.

Hotels

The hotel market is most developed in Bucharest, which has a range of facilities across all star categories. The larger towns and coastal resorts also have a fairly decent selection. At the higher end of the ranking system, the

The Intercontinental Hotel is the tallest building in the capital city

The Athénée Palace Hilton, formerly full of 'spies, political conspirators, adventurers, concession hunters, and financial manipulators'

hotels have everything you'd expect. Lower down, though, the star system becomes less reliable, with 3-star facilities and below often hit and miss. Places along the Black Sea coast, full of Romanians throughout summer regardless of the quality of facilities and service, can be particularly disappointing. Accommodation options outside the main cities, which see few foreign visitors, can also be poor, insalubrious and noisy; the local nightclub is occasionally attached. Some establishments ask for payment up front, indicative of the trust placed in the clientele as well as the management's confidence in customer satisfaction. Some hotels, but not all, include breakfast in the room rate.

Prices are usually lower than in the West in all but the top hotels. However, they are still often higher than the general cheapness of travelling in Romania would suggest, and have been rising quickly in recent years. Tariffs vary greatly depending on the demand, time of year and location. Visitors to Bucharest are generally there for business rather than leisure, so reductions are more commonly offered over the weekend. It can sometimes be worth trying to negotiate a discount, particularly if there are few guests at the time.

Self-catering

An alternative to hotels in the larger cities is self-catering accommodation, typically an apartment with fairly modern furniture and amenities. These can often work out better value than hotels. An internet search for 'self-catering' or 'short-term rental' and the city you wish to visit should yield a decent selection.

Homestays

Cheaper and more informal than a hotel is the network of private rooms that the owners let out to tourists. At the organised end of things is ANTREC, the National Association of Rural, Ecological and Cultural Tourism (*www.antrec.ro*), which lists the details of official homestays and pensions on its website. But the majority of rooms to let in private homes are on offer either from unofficial agents who wait at the station for tourists to arrive by train or simply with a sign outside proclaiming *cazare* (accommodation). This kind of room can be a bargain, although standards vary greatly and rural pensions may have squat toilets, restricted (or no) hot water and an unreliable power supply. However, these must be set against the benefits of living in an authentic Romanian household, which affords an insight into the people and culture that is not otherwise possible (*see pp120–21 for more details*). Another branch of this style of accommodation is agrotourism, which offers beds in rural and remote locations (*see www.antrec.ro*).

Youth hostels

Romania's youth hostel network is developing but by no means comprehensive, with three dozen Hostelling International facilities

Homestays offer authentic Romanian accommodation

complemented by a few independent places. Bucharest has several, and you are likely to find a clutch in the larger cities and in places of interest to tourists. Compared to the unreliability of its hotels, the country's hostels can be surprisingly well equipped and welcoming, with friendly staff, internet access, a laundry and day trips arranged. Similar – though usually more austere – accommodation can sometimes be found in vacated student dorms in holiday time.

Cabanas

Catering largely to hikers are chalets, or cabanas, often basic facilities found in mountain areas with a simple restaurant. In some such places, you will find little in the way of comfort or luxury, which is reflected in the low prices. However, other chalets are more upmarket. As well as their convenient location, they serve as good places to pick up useful information about hiking trails. Booking ahead is seldom necessary, although some cabanas, particularly in the busier stop-off points, are popular. Even more basic are the unattended wooden huts, or refuges, that offer free respite to walkers in the wild.

Camping

Camping is possible throughout much of Romania, both in official sites and elsewhere, with the authorities generally tolerating campers providing they do not make a mess. The official sites come in two categories: first class, which often have cabins for rent, as well as decent wash facilities and a restaurant, and slightly grimmer second class, usually offering nothing more than some unappealing toilets. If you have a high level of tolerance, camping is a very cheap way to get off the beaten track in Romania. It's also popular with local people; camping on the beach at the Goa-esque resort of Vama Veche is something of a tradition with the young, alternative crowd, and you'll also see plenty of tents pitched around the Danube Delta (despite developers' designs to supplant camping with more upmarket accommodation). Remote mountain areas are another camping 'hotspot'.

Mountain hotels quickly fill up during ski and summer seasons

Food and drink

Romanian cuisine is much as the visitor would expect; meat-based, hearty country food with some Eastern European staples. But while it might lack sophistication, innovation and variety, a few gems and a wealth of tasty, organic produce make it worth venturing outside the many Italian restaurants that dominate the restaurant scene. Outside the main cities you will have to; foreign food has made few forays into the countryside.

Meals

Simple and filling, local food bears traces of the country's accommodation of Turkish, Balkan, Hungarian, German and Roman regimes. Many foreigners find the local food bland, as Romanians prefer to salt their meals heavily rather than incorporate exotic spices.

Meals often start with a tasty soup, or *ciorbă*, a thin liquid with the ingredients floating in it. Vegetable, chicken, bean and fish are some of the best. *Ciorbă de burtă*, a sour and garlicky tripe soup beloved of Romanians, who believe it cures hangovers, is more polarising.

Meat's scarcity under Communism has earned it a privileged position as the mainstay of any meal. Pork is the favourite for special occasions; beef and chicken are also popular, while lamb and fish are rarer. Vegetarians will struggle outside the capital's more modern restaurants.

Accompaniments include *mămăliguță* (polenta), bread, potatoes,

either as thin, salty chips or tasty *cartofi țărănești* (peasant potatoes with onions), and simple salads. Popular desserts are pancakes, pie and *papanași* (cheese doughnuts with jam and sour cream).

In restaurants, 10 per cent tips are acceptable.

Romania has some decent wines

Simple, country food, such as aubergine salad and soup, will be on offer

Romanian specialities

Foreigners often enjoy *salate de vinete*, grilled aubergine (eggplant) with onion. Another vegetable spread is *zacuscă*, which contains aubergine, pepper, onion and beans, while *sarmale*, traditional Christmas food and year-round favourite, are leaf rolls of mincemeat and rice. Both are found throughout the Balkans. The Romanian culinary institution of *mititei*, a ground meat sausage eaten with mustard, is popular in the summer at communal gatherings, usually washed down with beer.

Drinks

Alcohol is ubiquitous in Romanian culture, making its presence felt in everything from social occasions to folk songs. Home-brewed wine became a cheap way of forgetting the hard toil of rural life. Local wine has yet to wow world markets, but there are decent bottles to try, particularly reds. Romanians prefer sweet wines, and often mix white wine with sparkling water. Some not-so-good restaurants will bring you unchilled white wine – ask for ice.

But Romania is more of a beer country, and its lager, or *bere blonda*, is a bargain. The national spirit is *ţuică*, a bracing plum brandy. Romanians toast by saying '*noroc*' (for luck) or '*sanatate*' (for health), sometimes several times throughout the meal. It is considered bad luck to toast with someone who's not drinking alcohol, and Romanians will recoil dramatically rather than do so.

The term *suc* (juice) in Romania also incorporates carbonated soda; (expensive) fresh juice is *suc proaspat*. Another confusing term is *apa minerala*, which refers specifically to sparkling water; for still water, ask for *apa plata*.

Romanian coffee is Turkish-style – strong, sweet and with the dregs at the bottom. The country also has a marvellous range of herbal and plant teas.

Entertainment

Romania's cities have a flourishing cultural life, with active theatres, concert halls and independent music venues all staging high-quality entertainment for a fraction of the cost of the equivalent event in a Western country. Years of Communist oppression combined with the Latin spirit have left Romanians with a carpe diem *spirit evident in the club nights that see revellers dancing until the sun comes up. Outside the major towns, there are fewer options, with entertainment mostly coming in the form of a few drinks with companions.*

Romanians are fond of their coffee and cigarettes, and all larger cities have plenty of cafés to while away the time over an espresso and a smoke. These run the gamut from cheap, informal places where coffee is served through a hatch and consumed in the street by customers standing at waist-height round tables to plush lounge-style coffee shops with Western décor and prices. In recent years big names such as Starbucks and Costa Coffee have opened their first outlets in the capital, oases for non-smokers wanting to enjoy the city's café scene without a fug of fumes.

The restaurant scene, too, is changing rapidly. A few years ago foreign food meant Italian, decent Asian food was a distant dream and service was almost universally appalling. Bucharest now has a cornucopia of cuisines on offer, from the ubiquitous local restaurants and Italian *trattorie* to Japanese, Brazilian, fusion and a wealth of other gastronomies. Some eateries here would not be out of place in London or New York. Prices, while rising rapidly, will not dent Western wallets. Outside

A band plays in Cişmigiu, Bucharest

A classical concert at the Ateneul Român will delight both for the music and the venue

the capital, the larger cities have a few good places to dine, often in 4- and 5-star hotels. Smaller towns and rural hamlets offer solely local fare (with occasional attempts at pizza and pasta) in basic, uninspiring environs, but can still be pleasant places to pass the time, especially if they have outside tables in summer and a nice view.

Bars are a big part of the social scene. Like restaurants, they run the gamut from exclusive city clubs catering to the country's *fitosi* (poseurs) to no-frills drinking dens for workers, called *birturi*, selling beer and cheap vodka. Though the latter tend to be patronised solely by old men, they can be interesting places to pop into for a glimpse of the traditional culture if the atmosphere does not put you off.

Nights out get started late and go on and on; night clubs are often open (and sometimes still relatively full) until 5am. Many are smoky basement dives. While city nightlife is varied, featuring Irish bars, jazz clubs, fancy Western-style places and more traditional taverns, in smaller towns evening venues often resemble dismal youth clubs, with a few chairs and tables and some pub games, such as pool, plus antiquated video games.

With the dubbing of films giving way to the cheaper option of subtitles, the cinema is another good way to pass the time. Swanky (and costly) multiplexes are now cropping up, but more of a pleasure are the atmospheric Communist-era city cinemas, with their old-fashioned seats and shaky

A statue of George Enescu, the country's most renowned composer, in front of the Romanian Opera in Bucharest

projectors. Best of all are the few state-sponsored cinemas that show art films and classics – anything from 1920s German silent films to Agatha Christie adaptations. Be warned that some Romanians consider it perfectly normal to talk loudly during the show.

Other cultural events attract more respectful audiences. Romania's cultural life is now thriving again after five decades of Communism. Ballets, operas and classical music concerts are regularly staged in Bucharest, and many of the other major towns are also home to important theatres and cultural venues. Festivals showcasing music, film and theatre are also staged annually around the country, the biggest of which is probably the George Enescu International Festival (*see p19*), a biennial programme of classical music, ballet, exhibitions and films. Tickets to events will not set you back more than a few pounds. Big names from the world of pop music are now also starting to include Romania in their European tours, with George Michael, the Rolling Stones and the Black Eyed Peas all playing gigs in Bucharest in 2007. Tickets are again far cheaper than in Western Europe. All of these events are hugely popular with middle-class Romanians, who turn out in force.

On a smaller scale, clubs, cafés and bars also host their own live music, usually jazz or rock. To find out what is on, look for posters advertising major events, and check local listings guides, which are distributed free in hotels and restaurants: *Sapte Seri* and *24 Fun* are both comprehensive and have several regional and online editions (*www.sapteseri.ro* and *www.b24fun.ro*). What you may find lacking is the opportunity to see much in the way of traditional folk music; with a still limited tourism industry, Romania does not really package this for visitors yet in the way that some countries do. Your best chance of hearing local bands is probably in traditional Romanian restaurants, which sometimes have musicians going from table to table playing.

Tourists also have museums, which can sometimes be found in the unlikeliest of small villages, with which to occupy themselves. Some museums (and galleries, which are often referred to as 'art museums') are tiny, quirky places, staffed by one or two elderly workers who have probably been there since the opening. Others are large and modern, with inscriptions in English. All charge entrance fees. Some towns also have zoos, but a regard for animal rights has yet to penetrate Romania, and they tend to be dispiriting affairs.

Another popular pastime with local people is gambling. It is difficult to walk far in a large Romanian town without passing either a bookmaker, amusement arcade or a casino. Foreigners tend to gravitate towards the more upmarket venues, usually attached to a hotel or restaurant. These can be quite grand, although the preponderance of mini-skirted croupiers gives such places a seedy 1970s feel. The average Romanian punter spends his money at humbler outlets. More sports-oriented casinos show multiple foreign football matches simultaneously via overseas cable channels, which can be useful if you want to catch an important game. They sometimes offer subsidised food and drinks, too.

Bucharest's Teatrul Naţional hosts many cultural events

Shopping

While Romania cannot be considered a major shopping destination, the local craft industry yields some interesting souvenirs. They are on sale, at a premium, in tourist shops in the larger cities, but can often be bought at a better price direct from the manufacturer, or from an informal market stall. Such stalls are often clustered around the entrance to major tourist attractions, or at the sides of main inter-city roads.

Typical Romanian souvenirs come mostly from traditional peasant crafts. Embroidered fabrics, frilly tablecloths and red, stripy covers make easily transportable presents, although many designs may be a little fussy for Western tastes. Peasant-inspired tops and shirts are easy to track down, and have received a boost in desirability from the popularity of the 'boho' look in recent years. Hand-woven rugs are another option; these are sometimes on sale from men wandering around the streets of Bucharest. From time to time, organised fairs are held, where local manufacturers bring their wares into town. Bucharest's Village Museum sometimes hosts one such event shortly before Christmas. Keep an eye open for posters or check listings guides to see if anything coincides with your visit.

Romania also makes a range of decent, less transportable, breakables. Brightly coloured ceramics, pottery, glass and vases all offer fairly good value. Delicate painted eggs, on sale at various monasteries, are a great example of local folk art. Another religious souvenir is the painted icons, available in the little shops housed in the larger churches. To export genuine religious art, rather than inexpensive reproductions, you need permission from the church authorities in

Rustic pottery makes a charming memento of your trip

Be prepared for some tough haggling at the country's markets

Bucharest (*Bulevardul Coşbuc. Tel: (021) 337 4031*).

If you're after something a little more individual, Bucharest's Lipscani district is home to several quirky antiques shops, where Bakelite telephones, old typewriters and Communist memorabilia are some of the more everyday wares. The other large towns have similar shops, though fewer of them.

From the old to the very new, Romania has recently started to embrace the shopping mall. The country's first official one, Bucureşti Mall, a bizarre-looking pink construction, opened in 1999 (shopping centres existed previously but Romanians refuse to count them as malls). Since then, developers have been scrambling to add more. Most are

not worth visiting for the shopping; imported Western goods cost more in Romania than you'd pay at home. But as a glimpse of the country's nouveau riche (many young people dress up for mall outings) and the results of a rapid transition from Communism to Capitalism, they are fascinating. At the other end of the scale are markets, where you can pick up gifts such as honey or locally made wine.

Outside its malls, Bucharest's main shopping streets are Bulevardul Magheru (high-street stores) and Calea Victoriei (high-end and designer boutiques); in Braşov go to Strada Republicii and Strada Mureşenilor; and in Constanţa try Strada Ştefan cel Mare, in particular the pedestrianised area. In the smaller towns the shops are concentrated in the centre.

Sport and leisure

Sport in Romania tends to mean football. Supporters are passionate about their clubs and the national side. Despite having some talented players (Gheorghe Hagi is the best known), the potential of the sport in the country has been largely squandered, as the game is generally run by disreputable businessmen with little expertise. However, if you don't mind the decaying stadiums, a game can be an enjoyable spectacle, enlivened by voluble supporters.

The season runs from August to December, with a winter break, and then from March to June. Games take place on Friday, Saturday and Sunday evenings, weekend afternoons and occasionally on a Wednesday night. Tickets, which are very cheap, are on sale from small offices at the ground before the game. If you can't go to the ground, watching a match in a bar is also a colourful and atmospheric experience.

There are few opportunities for the casual visitor to play football. But Romania's great outdoors yields plenty of other activities. Though not particularly high, the Carpathians offer hikers varied and impressive scenery, including gorges, valleys and rock formations. Trails are marked with coloured symbols and on maps. Serious walkers can book all-inclusive holidays, or head off with camping gear. Others can take a cable car (*telecabina* or *telegondola*) up to the top and enjoy the view at a restaurant or on a brief stroll.

The other main purpose of going to the mountains is skiing (*see pp60–61 for details*). Romania is improving its ski resorts and, providing you do not

More demanding sports are also gaining in popularity

Romanians enjoy a game of beach volleyball

demand luxury, the skiing is not bad value. The main hub is the Prahova Valley resorts, but there are a few others around the country. Most of the slopes are more suited to novices, but there are a few runs for the very advanced. Ski season generally lasts from late November to March, but Romanian weather can be erratic so it does vary. Equipment can be hired from various outlets at the foot of the mountains; you'll need to produce a passport.

The third mountain pastime, though far less common than the other two, is caving. Romania has over 12,000 caves. Some of the best are in the Apuseni mountains. Again, where you go will depend on how proficient you

are; there are caves suited to mainstream groups of tourists right up to more exigent crevices for experts only. Serious cavers can contact the **Emil Racoviță Institute of Speleology** (*Clinicilor 5, Cluj. Tel: (0264) 595 954. www.speleological-institute-cluj.org*).

Mountain tracks are also home to bikers. The Bucegi mountains, by Prahova Valley, are the most popular place for mountain biking. Bikes can be hired in some resorts, from where you can take the cable car up to the top with your cycle. A hostel or hotel may be able to assist you with bike hire. Cycling in towns and villages is less of a pleasure due to the uneven road surfaces and stray dogs, packs of

Bungee jumping at Izvor Park

whom often pursue passing cyclists for fun. Romania has several cycling clubs, including the **Clubul de Cicloturism Napoca** (*Tel: (0264) 450 013*).

Romania's pleasant countryside can also be enjoyed on horseback. Equine enthusiasts can take a tailor-made horse trek for several days through the Carpathians, a marvellous way to get off the beaten track and see remote Romania. For dabblers, there are also horse-riding clubs on the outskirts of various towns, including Bucharest.

Golf has only just begun to take off in Romania, spurred by the influx of foreign businessmen as the economy has grown. Currently there is just one nine-hole course, Lac de Verde in the Prahova Valley, but an 18-hole course near Braşov is expected to be ready in 2009, with several more in the pipeline over the next five years. Bucharest also has some facilities. The **Romanian**

GHEORGHE HAGI

Gheorghe Hagi, or the 'Maradona of the Carpathians', as he was nicknamed, is the country's greatest footballing legend and its top-scoring player. Hagi represented Romania in three World Cups and three European Football Championships, but achieved worldwide recognition in the 1994 World Cup. That year saw Romania deliver its best international performance, reaching the quarter finals. Hagi scored three goals en route, including a 37-m (121-ft) lob over the Colombian goalkeeper that went down as one of the goals of the tournament. While his subsequent managerial career has been less illustrious, Hagi remains a local hero.

Golf Federation is a useful resource (*Strada Carierei 44, Breaza, Prahova. Tel: (0344) 814 756 or 0727 770 987. www.romaniangolffederation.com*).

The delta – Europe's most important wetland – is Romania's main bird-watching hub, home to numerous different species of resident and migratory birds (*see pp72–3*). The best times to see them are between the end of March and June (especially May) and then from August to October. Pelicans, cormorants, herons and falcons are just a few of the highlights. Aside from the delta, the mountains and lowland deciduous forests are also rich in bird life. Fishing is another popular pastime at the delta (with over 160 species present) and elsewhere throughout the country.

The Black Sea coast is home to a small but growing water-sports industry, currently just enough to provide an occasional diversion from lying on the beach. Boat trips, scuba-diving, windsurfing, waterskiing, kayaking, canoeing and banana boating are possible. Informal operators conduct their business from the beach itself. There is also the **Romanian Sailing Federation** (*www.sailing.ro*) and the **Royal Romanian Yacht Club** (*www.ycrr.ro*).

Parts of the coast, as well as other spots around Romania, are also renowned for their spa resorts, of which the country has 160, as well as a third of Europe's mineral springs. Different resorts cater for different health complaints – gynaecological, cardiovascular, digestive, nervous and so on. Local researchers have even been involved in drugs said to reverse the aging process, although you may have some doubts as to their efficacy. In general, treatment involves drinking the local water, taking mud baths and undergoing complementary therapies, and a full course can take upwards of a couple of weeks (*see pp118–19*). If you're looking for something quicker, many city beauty parlours and gyms also offer massages, although if you see massage advertised, it's worth making sure what kind of establishment you're about to enter.

Steaua Bucureşti is the country's most popular team

Children

Cheap, child-friendly and with the whole Dracula phenomenon, Romania can be a good – if not the most obvious – place to take the family. Exploring spooky Transylvanian castles is sure to excite children, and there is also the chance to get up close to wildlife, take boat trips, creep through caves and be scared by Dracula himself. On the downside, you'll face a lack of facilities, a surfeit of cigarette smoke and your children's sad bewilderment at seeing street kids of their own age.

Coastal holidays are an obvious place to start. Messing around in the sand and sea is always entertaining for younger children. Keep a close eye on your children in the water though; some resorts have lifeguards but their professionalism and efficacy is open to question. A larger resort like Mamaia is a better choice for families, as there will be plenty of seaside entertainments such as catapult or reverse bungee, mini-boating lakes and race tracks, clowns and balloon sellers. Aqua parks, which can be found in the larger cities as well as by the sea, are another ideal way to occupy the kids on a hot day.

Romania's vast countryside also has a lot for slightly older children, such as horse-riding, mountain biking and quad biking. Even younger holiday-makers can enjoy exploring quirky caves and taking a ride on a horse and cart. The great outdoors will also bring children into contact with the country's rich wildlife. Whether it is bird-spotting on a boat trip around the delta or watching bears forage though the Braşov bins from the safety of your car, children will enjoy a proximity to animals that they would otherwise only get in a zoo.

Children are well catered for at the seaside

Aqua Magic, a large water park in Mamaia, the best coastal resort to take the kids

The other main draw for children is, obviously, Dracula. Transylvanian castles may have had little connection with Vlad Țepeș, and even less with the fictional vampire he inspired, but that will not spoil the fun of the Gothic castles and masks and other kitsch on sale in all tourist towns. For closer interaction with the count himself (well, an actor doing a passable impression), the twice-weekly show at the **Count Dracula Club restaurant** (*Splaiul Independenței 8a. Tel: (021) 312 13 53. www.count-dracula.ro. Open: Mon–Sat 3pm–1am. Closed: Sun. Metro: Piața Unirii*) in Bucharest is unmissable if you have older children; younger ones may well start screaming.

Actual things that children might need – high chairs, children's menus, baby-changing facilities in toilets – are almost entirely lacking in Romania, but there is no need to worry about Romania's past reputation for lack of absolute essentials. These days everything you need will be available in city supermarkets and hypermarkets, although it is sensible to stock up before heading off for a few days in rural areas. Wherever you go, you will find Romanians child-friendly. Local children are indulged rather than disciplined; your toddler could be screaming its head off in an upmarket restaurant and the only tutting would probably be coming from fellow foreigners.

Essentials

Arriving
By air
Flight possibilities to Romania are increasing all the time, including low-cost options. There are direct flights to and from most major airports in Europe, as well as Dubai, Tel Aviv and Istanbul. Non-stop flights to New York may be reintroduced.

Passengers flying into Bucharest will land at either Otopeni (officially Henri Coandă International Airport although nobody seems to call it that), a 20- to 30-minute drive from the city centre, or Baneasa, which is nearer to the centre of town.

All offers of a taxi at either airport should be firmly rejected, the only cab firm allowed to pick up passengers being the expensive Fly Taxi. It is better to phone another firm (*see below*) and book a car; you will then have to cross the road outside the terminal and wait for it in the carpark. An even cheaper option is the 783 bus, which leaves every 15–30 minutes between 5.30am and 11pm from outside the domestic terminal. Buy your ticket beforehand from the kiosk.

Bucharest taxi firms (prefix with *021* if calling from a mobile):

Confort *Tel: 9455*
Leone *Tel: 9425*
Meridian *Tel: 9444*
Taxi 2000 *Tel: 9494*

By bus
There is no coach station as such in Bucharest; most buses drop off opposite the Gara de Nord.

By car
The best place to enter Romania by car when coming from Western Europe is Battonya-Turnu, which is free from lorry traffic. Major border crossings are open non-stop.

By rail
Inter-railers are likely to arrive at the Gara de Nord in Bucharest. The station has improved since people were charged to enter it (you don't have to pay if you have a rail ticket) but it still attracts dubious characters; on no account take a taxi from outside as the drivers there are the worst crooks in the industry. The same applies at the regional stations.

Customs
With Romania a European Union member since the start of 2007, you are now theoretically allowed to import and export without restriction to and from other member states. Non-EU citizens can enter and leave the country with up to US$10,000 in cash or travellers' cheques, import 200 cigarettes or 40 cigars, 4 litres of wine or 2 of spirits, 20 rolls of camera film, 'reasonable amounts' of gifts and medicine for personal use.

Electricity

The supply is at 220–240V, 50Hz. Romanian plug sockets are the two-round-pin kind found throughout continental Europe, so you will need an adaptor if you want to use any British appliances.

Internet

Romania has plenty of internet cafés in all major cities and a few in smaller towns. The speed, frustratingly slow in the past, is improving quickly. A growing number of top hotels and restaurants now have Wi-Fi access, too.

Money

The Romanian currency is the lei. The old lei (ROL) recently lost four zeroes to become the new lei (RON) to align the currency to the euro, which Romania hopes ultimately to adopt.

Banks and ATMs

There are plenty of places to change money, from bureaux de change to banks; take your passport. You should not be charged any commission, except for travellers' cheques. Copious ATMs (*bancomaturi*) can be found in Bucharest and other larger cities, although some have an aversion to foreign cards.

Credit cards

Credit card acceptance is widespread in major towns, but rare in villages, with the exception of higher-ranked hotels.

Opening hours

Shops typically open 9am–6pm or 8pm and tend to remain closed altogether on Sunday (outside the main shopping districts of large towns and malls). Offices and banks seldom open over the weekend at all and usually close by 5pm, sometimes 4pm. Large post offices are usually open until 8pm, 2pm on Saturday.

Passports and visas

EU passport holders can come and go with just a valid passport. If your proposed stay is longer than 90 days, you will need to get a registration certificate from the Ministry of Foreign Affairs. US, Canadian, Australian, New Zealand and South African tourists can also stay visa-free for up to 90 days.

Pharmacies

Romania has well-stocked, modern pharmacies (*farmacie*), and you should find at least one 24-hour one in each major area. Most pharmacists speak at least a little English. If you're heading for a rural or remote area, stock up on supplies before you leave.

Post

Post offices in Romania can be found in almost every town. Posting a parcel involves reams of bureaucracy. Letters take about five days to Western Europe, a couple of weeks to the US and Australasia. Items occasionally go astray, so if you're sending something important, use recorded delivery.

Public holidays

1–2 Jan	New Year
6 Jan	Epiphany
Mar–May	Orthodox Easter (Monday is a bank holiday, not Friday)
1 May	Labour Day
1 Dec	National Day
25–26 Dec	Christmas

Smoking

EU law has resulted in the grudging establishment of non-smoking areas in restaurants and cafés, but these are seldom properly segregated from the smoky main section. In general, the more upmarket the venue, the greater likelihood of being able to avoid smoke.

Suggested reading and media

The most obvious choice is *Dracula* by Bram Stoker. *The Balkan Trilogy* by Olivia Manning is also recommended. Dennis Deletant and Nicolae Klepper are names to look out for on the non-fiction side.

You will never be short of English-language television. Almost everybody has cable packages, which include the BBC and CNN. The BBC World Service broadcasts on FM in Bucharest (88FM) and Timişoara (93.9FM). English-language print press is limited mostly to the larger cities. *Bucharest In Your Pocket* is an excellent bi-monthly listings magazine, and there are other free publications of varying quality which are distributed in hotels and restaurants. Though in Romanian, *Şapte Seri* and *24 Fun* are useful and comprehensive listings magazines.

Tax

If you buy anything expensive in Romania you are entitled to claim back the VAT. Ask for a store-identified VAT Refund form, and take it, with the receipt, to the VAT refund office at the border/airport.

Telephones

Romania has plenty of card-operated payphones; the cards are on sale in supermarkets and newsagents. If you're staying longer and are planning to make a lot of calls, there are discount cards available for calling abroad. Another option for long-term visitors is to have your mobile unlocked (which can be done cheaply when you arrive) and buy a local SIM card. For a short stay, your own mobile would suffice for sending a few texts. Coverage is fairly good throughout the country.

To call any number in Romania from abroad, dial the international code, *4*, for Romania and the number.

Note that from May 2008, all numbers will be prefixed by an area code, no matter where you're calling from within the country.

Directory Assistance Service *931*
International Operator *971*

To call abroad from Romania dial *0* plus the relevant country code:

Australia *61*   **Canada** *1*
Ireland *353*   **New Zealand** *64*
South Africa *27*   **UK** *44*
USA *1*

Time zone

Romania is two hours ahead of the UK, seven ahead of East Coast America and ten ahead of West Coast America. Australia is between five and seven hours ahead; New Zealand nine.

Toilets

City toilets are generally decent, although in downmarket places the seats can get dirty. Hotels and restaurants are usually obliging if you ask to use their facilities. The plumbing can be second-rate, and you will often see signs asking you to put toilet paper into a bin rather than flush it.

Travellers with disabilities

Romania has some way to go before travellers with disabilities can enjoy a relatively stress-free holiday there. Only the better hotels and some spa resorts give any thought to the needs of those with limited mobility. Manic and hazardous driving, parked cars that block the pavements and pot-holed and uneven surfaces are a few of the obstacles put in front of the traveller with disabilities, and public transport is almost entirely off limits. More positively, Romanians are generally very helpful to foreign visitors.

Essentials

CONVERSION TABLE

FROM	TO	MULTIPLY BY
Inches	Centimetres	2.54
Feet	Metres	0.3048
Yards	Metres	0.9144
Miles	Kilometres	1.6090
Acres	Hectares	0.4047
Gallons	Litres	4.5460
Ounces	Grams	28.35
Pounds	Grams	453.6
Pounds	Kilograms	0.4536
Tons	Tonnes	1.0160

To convert back, for example from centimetres to inches, divide by the number in the third column.

MEN'S SUITS

UK	36	38	40	42	44	46	48
Rest of Europe	46	48	50	52	54	56	58
USA	36	38	40	42	44	46	48

DRESS SIZES

UK	8	10	12	14	16	18
France	36	38	40	42	44	46
Italy	38	40	42	44	46	48
Rest of Europe	34	36	38	40	42	44
USA	6	8	10	12	14	16

MEN'S SHIRTS

UK	14	14.5	15	15.5	16	16.5	17
Rest of Europe	36	37	38	39/40	41	42	43
USA	14	14.5	15	15.5	16	16.5	17

MEN'S SHOES

UK	7	7.5	8.5	9.5	10.5	11
Rest of Europe	41	42	43	44	45	46
USA	8	8.5	9.5	10.5	11.5	12

WOMEN'S SHOES

UK	4.5	5	5.5	6	6.5	7
Rest of Europe	38	38	39	39	40	41
USA	6	6.5	7	7.5	8	8.5

Language

Romanian is a Latin language, and anyone who studied French or Spanish at school will be able to have a stab at translating some words; Italian is even more similar. In the cities, English is widely spoken, particularly by young people. In rural areas, those involved in the tourist trade will know at least a smattering, but few others will.

PRONUNCIATION

â/î = oo as in look

ă = e as in the

c = ch

i = very slightly pronounced at the end of a word

ş = sh

ţ = ts as in cats

NUMBERS

1	unu	(oo-noo)
2	doi	(doy)
3	trei	(tray)
4	patru	(patroo)
5	cinci	(chinch)
6	şase	(shasay)
7	şapte	(shaptay)
8	opt	(opt)
9	nouă	(no-wah)
10	zece	(zeh-chay)
20	douăzeci	(doh-wah-zech)
100	o sută	(oh soo-tah)
1000	o mie	(oh mee-yay)

GREETINGS AND POLITENESS

Thank you	Mulţumesc	(Moolt-zoo-mesc)
You're welcome	Cu plăcere	(Koo plah-chair-ay)
Please	Vă rog	(Vuh rog)
Excuse me	Mă scuzaţi	(Muh skoo-zats)
Hello	Bună ziua	(Boo-nuh zee-wuh)
Goodbye	La revedere, Pa	(Lah rev-er-dare-ay, Pah)
Good morning	Bună dimineaţa	(Boo-nuh dim-in-ee-atsa)
Good day	Bună ziua	(Boo-nuh zee-wuh)
Good evening	Bună seara	(Boo-nuh sarah)
Good night	Noapte bună	(Nowaptah boo-nuh)

EVERYDAY EXPRESSIONS

Yes	Da	(*dar*)
No	Nu	(*noo*)
There is / There are	Este/Sunt	(*yes-tay/soont*)
Where is?	Unde e	(*oonday eh*)
When?	Când	(*cuhnd*)
How long?	Cât timp	(*cuht timp*)
I want	Vreau	(*vrow*)
How much is this?	Cât costat	(*cuht cost't*)
Expensive	Scump	(*scoomp*)
Cheap	Ieftin	(*yef-tin*)
Money	Bani	(*ban*)
May I have the bill please?	Notă de plată, vă rog	(*note-uh de platter vuh rog*)
Where is the toilet?	Unde e toaleta?	(*oonday eh toy-a-letter*)
Do you speak English?	Vorbiți engleză?	(*vor-beets en-glaze-uh*)

TIME

Yesterday	Ieri	(*yeah-r*)
Today	Azi	(*azz*)
Tomorrow	Mâine	(*moy-nuh*)
What time is it?	Cât este ora/ceasul	(*cuht yestay or-ah/chassul*)

DAYS OF THE WEEK

Monday	Luni	(*loon*)
Tuesday	Marți	(*marts*)
Wednesday	Miercuri	(*mee-yeah-cure*)
Thursday	Joi	(*zhoi*)
Friday	Vineri	(*vin-air*)
Saturday	Sâmbătă	(*suhm-but-uh*)
Sunday	Duminică	(*doo-min-i-cuh*)

Emergencies

Emergency numbers

All-purpose number	*112*
Ambulance	*973*
Fire	*981*
Police	*955*

Central Police Station, Bucharest
(021) 311 2021

Medical services
Casualty and doctors

All major cities have large hospitals, which, though the facilities may look a little primitive, generally have excellent staff. Rumours circulate about doctors demanding bribes before they will treat patients but this, though not impossible, is exaggerated. Most doctors speak good English. Smaller towns have fewer facilities. There are a number of very professional private clinics, again, mostly in the big cities. You will also find opticians and dentists in most major towns.

Pharmacies

All large towns have well-stocked pharmacies, although you may have to venture further afield to find one if you're staying in a small village or particularly remote spot. Modern and reliable chains include Sensiblu and Help Net. In Bucharest and the larger cities you will find several pharmacies that are open 24 hours a day.

Health risks and insurance

The tap water is safe to drink, and most cafés and restaurants have decent hygiene standards.

Romania has a reciprocal health agreement with the UK, USA, Canada and Australia. UK citizens get free treatment with a European Health Insurance Card, available from UK post offices. Citizens of other countries will have to pay cash for their treatment at the time. Simple procedures are not usually terribly expensive. Everybody will have to pay for any drugs they are prescribed. Health insurance is highly recommended.

Safety and crime

Despite the negative associations, Romania is a relatively safe place to travel. Crime is typically of the petty, non-violent variety. Watch out for pickpockets in public places.

Don't believe anyone who describes himself as 'tourist police'. And don't be tempted to exchange money in the street. With this in mind and common sense, your holiday is likely to be trouble-free.

There are a couple of hazards to watch out for. The first is the traffic as Romania has an abysmal road safety record.

Another issue is stray dogs. While mainly a nuisance rather than a danger, they do sometimes bite. It is better to avoid deserted streets where they tend to congregate. Rabies is very rare, but if a bite breaks the skin it may be worth having it checked out.

Embassies and consulates
Romanian embassies abroad
Australia
4 Dalman Crescent O'Malley
ACT 2606 Canberra
Tel: (026) 286 2343

Canada
655 Rideau Street
Ottawa, ON, K1N 6A3
Tel: (613) 789 3709

Ireland
6 Waterloo Road
Dublin 4
Tel: (01) 668 1085

New Zealand doesn't have a
Romanian Embassy.

South Africa
117 Charles Street, Brooklyn, 0181
Hatfield, 0028 Pretoria
Tel: (012) 4606941

UK
4 Palace Green, London W8 4QD
Tel: (020) 7937 9666

US
1607–23rd Street NW, Washington DC
20008. Tel: (202) 2323694

Foreign embassies and consulates in Romania
Australian Consulate General
World Trade Center, 10 Montreal
Square, Bucharest.
Tel: (021) 316 7558.

Canadian Embassy
Strada Nicolae Iorga 36, Bucharest.
Tel: (021) 307 5000.

Irish Consulate
Strada Vasile Lascăr 42–44, Bucharest.
Tel: (021) 212 2136.

New Zealand does not have
an embassy in Romania. New
Zealanders should contact the
British Embassy.

South African Embassy
Union International Business,
Stirbei Voda 26–28, Bucharest.
Tel: (021) 313 3725.

UK Embassy
Strada Jules Michelet 24, Bucharest.
Tel: (021) 201 7300.

US Embassy
Strada Tudor Arghezi 7–9,
Bucharest. Tel: (021) 200 3300.

Police
If you are the victim of a crime, report
it to the police. There's little chance of
their apprehending the culprit, but you
may need a crime number to make an
insurance claim. Romanian police have
a terrible reputation for corruption and
ineptitude, but the force has been
improving, and many officers are
now professional and courteous,
especially to foreigners. They are
easily identifiable, with blue uniforms
and hats.

Directory

Accommodation price guide

Prices are based on a double room per night for two people, usually with breakfast, in high season.

★	Under 110 RON
★★	110 RON–190 RON
★★★	190 RON–260 RON
★★★★	Over 260 RON

Eating out price guide

Prices are based on an average three-course meal for one, without drinks.

★	Under 25 RON
★★	25 RON–40 RON
★★★	40 RON–55 RON
★★★★	Over 55 RON

BUCHAREST

ACCOMMODATION

Youth Hostel Villa Helga ★★

YHI hostel in a pleasant area not far from the centre. The garden and picnic table are great in summer, and breakfast and laundry are included in the price.
Strada Mihai Eminescu 184. Tel: (021) 212 0828 or 0741 127 514. Email: villa_helga@yahoo.com. www.rotravel.com/hotels/helga

Ibis Palatul Parlamentului ★★★

Reliable and great-value hotel with disabled access. This recent addition to the international Ibis chain has a better location, close to the People's Palace and Izvor Park, than the first one, which is beside the Gara de Nord. Though not large, the rooms are comfortable and the bathrooms decent.
Strada Izvor 82–84. Tel: (021) 401 1000. Email: reservations@ibistel.com. www.ibishotel.com

Rembrandt ★★★★

One of Bucharest's most tasteful hotels, with wooden floors, large beds and classic furniture, this place exudes European elegance. The Rembrandt also has an unbeatable location in the city's historical centre. The small touches, like the CD player in every room, set things off. The lack of disabled access and parking space are the only downsides.
Strada Smardan 11. Tel: (021) 313 9315. Email: info@rembrandt.ro. www.rembrandt.ro

EATING OUT

Bistro Atheneu ★★

Right opposite the Athenaeum, this place is popular with foreigners who want to go local but not too local. It's a little dark inside, but the food is reliable and the interior décor (musical instruments on the walls

and a small fountain)
quaint.
Strada Episcopiei 2.
Tel: (021) 313 4900.
Open: daily noon–
midnight.

Caru' Cu Bere ★★

The century-old inn
Caru' Cu Bere (literally
'Cart with Beer') has
one of the most
spectacular restaurant
interiors in the country,
with high, ornate ceilings
and marvellous murals.
A recent management
change has also
improved the standards
of food (traditional
Romanian) and service,
although the interior
remains the big draw.
It can get busy during
peak hours, so call
ahead.
Strada Stavropoleos 3–5.
Tel: (021) 313 7560.
Open: daily 9am–
midnight.

Trattoria il Calcio ★★★

The four Bucharest
restaurants that make up
this chain might have the
atmosphere of a fast-
food joint at times, but
the Italian food is
superb, and the
introduction of non-
smoking sections has

made them a pleasanter
place to dine. Other
outlets are at Herăstrău
Park and Floreasca.
Strada Mendeleev 14.
Tel: 0722 134 299.
www.trattoriailcalcio.ro.
Open: Sun–Thur noon–
midnight, Fri & Sat
noon–1am. Closed: Mon.

Balthazar ★★★★

Top-class eatery serving
French-Asian fusion
food in a chic
environment. It's not
cheap by local standards,
but for this level of
quality in Western
Europe you'd probably
pay double.
Strada Dumbrava Roşie
2. Tel: (021) 310 7359.
www.balthazar.ro.
Open: daily noon–
midnight or last customer.

ENTERTAINMENT

Ateneul Român

The city's most
handsome building is also
an active venue, with
evening and occasional
morning concerts. The
high-quality musical
performance will have to
vie with the superlative
interior for your attention.
Strada Franklin 1.
Tel: (021) 315 2567,

ticket reservations
(021) 315 6875.
www.fge.org.ro

Cinema Pro

Large, plush and
comfortable, Cinema
Pro is the best modern
cinema in the city.
It's also very central,
just a couple of minutes
from Piaţa Universităţii.
The programme
consists of the latest
releases.
Strada Ion Ghica 3.
Tel: (031) 824 1360.

Club A

The student union
atmosphere makes a
welcome change from
many Bucharest clubs,
where the point is
looking good rather than
having fun. Expect a
strange but fun mix of
indie tunes and the odd
Romanian classic.
Strada Blănari 14.
Tel: (021) 313 5592.
www.cluba.ro

Green Hours

One of the city's most
civilised entertainment
venues, with jazz, live
theatre and other events
of a literary bent taking
place regularly. In
summer, the secluded
Green Hours terrace is

marvellous for long evenings drinking and chatting.
Calea Victoriei 120.
Tel: (021) 314 5751.
www.green-hours.ro
La Motoare
The open-air rooftop section of Lăptăria Enache, the bar at the top of the National Theatre, is hugely popular with young groups of Bucharest students. Occasional art exhibitions add to the trendy atmosphere.
Bulevardul Nicolae Bălcescu 2.
Tel: (021) 315 8508.
www.laptaria.totalnet.ro
National Opera House
Bucharest's imposing National Opera House stages regular ballets and operas. The quality of the productions is always high, and the tickets are an absolute bargain, even if the building's interior has seen better days. Tickets are on sale every day from the box office 10am–noon and, if any remain unsold, before performances.
Bulevardul Mihail Kogalniceanu 70–72.

Tel: (021) 314 6980.
www.operanb.ro
National Theatre
The majority of the productions here are staged in Romanian, which may render them of limited interest to foreigners. But the venue's three halls do from time to time play host to musical events as well. Tickets can be bought on site between 10am and 7pm (until 4pm on Mondays).
Bulevardul Nicolae Bălcescu 2.
Tel: (021) 314 7171.
Sala Union
State-sponsored cinema that broadcasts an impressive range of cultural and classic features. One day it could be early German silent film, the next *The Magnificent Seven.* Its sister cinema is Eforie, on Strada Eforie.
Strada Campineanu 21.
Tel: (021) 313 9289.

Hipocan
One of the city's most established riding schools, Hipocan organises competitions

and lessons. It is situated close to the main airport.
DJ101, Comuna Corbeanca, Ilfov.
Tel: (021) 266 6110.
Email: hipocan@as.ro.
www.hipocan.ro
Steaua Bucureşti FC
The country's most successful football club (they were the first team from Eastern Europe to win the European Cup in 1986, and remain the only Romanian club to have done so). Tickets can usually be bought at the ground before the match; only very big games sell out in advance.
Bulevardul Ghencea 45.
Tel: (021) 411 4656.
www.steauafc.com

THE PRAHOVA VALLEY
Azuga
ACCOMMODATION
Hotel Azuga EUR ★★
Widely considered the best place to stay in the town, Hotel Azuga has singles, doubles and triples and also accepts pets. The hotel restaurant is also probably your best bet for eating.

Strada Victoriei 87.
Tel: (0244) 327 406.

Buşteni
ACCOMMODATION
Hotel Silva ★★
Quiet rooms with
balconies, some afford
gorgeous mountain
views.
Strada Telecabinei 24.
Tel: (0244) 320 027.
www.hotelsilva.ro

EATING OUT
**Ristorante Falco
Bianco ★★**
This Italian-run
trattoria-style restaurant
serves a wide range of
pizza and pasta, and
can even rustle up food
from other national
cuisines if given a
day's notice.
Bulevardul Libertăţii
109. Tel: (0244) 320 347.
www.falcobianco.uv.ro.
Open: Mon–Thur 10am–
9pm, Fri–Sun 10am–
midnight.

Predeal
ACCOMMODATION
Hotel Carmen ★★
Not the most modern of
venues by any means,
but this well-equipped
hotel close to the station

offers guests plenty of
things to do, including
sauna, massage, gym,
table tennis, billiards and
disco-bar.
Bulevardul Mihail
Săulescu 121.
Tel: (0268) 456 656.

EATING OUT
Căprioara ★
Well-regarded Italian
eatery with a terrace and
ample parking.
Bulevardul Libertăţii 90.
Tel: (0268) 456 964.
Mama Maria ★★
Traditional Romanian
restaurant whose
papanasi (cheese-filled
doughnuts) get
particularly good
reviews.
Strada Eminescu 28.
Tel: (0268) 456 650.
Open: Wed–Mon 11am–
11pm.

ENTERTAINMENT
The Office
One of the most 'in'
night spots in Bucharest
over the last decade,
The Office now has two
clubs in the Prahova
Valley, the other being
in Sinaia. Expect
poseurs, high prices
and cool vibes.

Libertăţii Street No 108.
Tel: 0745 110 064.
www.theoffice.ro

SPORT AND LEISURE
Lac de Verde Golf Club
The country's first golf
course to speak of
currently has 9 holes, but
there are plans to extend
it to 18. Other activities
on offer at the facility
include horse-riding,
paintball, quad biking
and archery.
Strada Carierei 44,
Breaza.
Tel: (0244) 343 525.
Email:
contact@lacdeverde.ro.
www.lacdeverde.ro

Sinaia
ACCOMMODATION
Hotel Cerbul ★
Plain but respectable
accommodation in
between the post office
and the station. The
main reason to stay
here is the reasonable
price. Some rooms
have shared bathroom
facilities.
Bulevardul Carol I 19.
Tel: (0244) 312 391.
Email:
rezervari@cerbul.ro.
www.cerbul.ro

Hotel Păltiniş ★★

The non-smoking floor and the slightly ominous Brâncovenesc, castle-like design are two of the plus points of this traditional mountain hotel.
Bulevardul Carol I 67.
Tel: (0244) 314 651.
Email: rezervari@
hotelpaltinis.ro.
www.hotelpaltinis.ro

EATING OUT
Hotel Palace ★★

The hotel, now approaching the end of its first century in business, offers a stylish, traditional dining experience. Guests are seated in one of three large rooms and offered a varied menu featuring both Romanian and more international options.
Strada Octavian Goga
11. Tel: (0244) 312 051.
Email: scpalacesa@fx.ro
Taverna Sarbului ★★★

Excellent Serbian-run country restaurant, easily one of the best places to eat in Sinaia (unless you're vegetarian). The rustic décor, with plenty of wood and a log fire, is spot on, the service is good, there's a non-

smoking room and the portions are huge. Highly recommended.
Calea Codrului (en route
to Cota 1400).
Tel: (0244) 314 400.
www.tavernasarbului.ro.
Open: daily noon–11pm.

ENTERTAINMENT
Blue Angel

One of the city's most popular night-time venues, the Blue Angel can often get lively. The disco continues until 4am, and there is also billiards and table tennis for non-dancers.
Bulevardul Carol I 41.
Tel: (0244) 313 455.

SPORT AND LEISURE
New Montana Health Club and Spa

As well as a spa, pool, Jacuzzi® and various alternative therapies, this hotel also hires out decent ski equipment.
Bulevardul Carol I 24.
Tel: (0244) 312 751.
www.newmontana.ro
Snow

This ski and other sports equipment rental outlet also has a restaurant, which is particularly

pretty in summer thanks to the impressive floral displays.
Strada Cuza Voda.
Tel: (0244) 311 198.

TRANSYLVANIA
Bran
ACCOMMODATION
Vila Bran ★★

A complex of 11 buildings totalling over 100 rooms and two restaurants, Vila Bran is a lively place with mini-golf, horse-riding, basketball court, DJ nights and karaoke. Rooms are basic but perfectly acceptable, and the view of Bran Castle, the town's *raison d'être*, is excellent.
Strada Sohodol 271A.
Tel: (0268) 236 866 or
0722 485 407.
www.vilabran.ro

EATING OUT
Castelul Bran Cabana ★★

One of the better options for eating at the surprisingly poorly served Bran, this place specialises in local fare.
600m (656 yds) from
castle entrance.
Tel: (0268) 236 404.

Braşov

ACCOMMODATION

Kismet Dao ★

Located in the Schei district, to the south of the main sights, this hostel has both dormitory accommodation and private rooms. With jovial staff, video games and a good selection of local trips available, it's a good choice if you appreciate a youth hostel atmosphere.
Strada Democratiei 2.
Tel: (0268) 514 296.
www.kismetdao.com

Tineret ADABelle ★★★

A hostel-style facility (*tineret* means 'youth' in Romanian), this central place prides itself on giving value for money; room rates include both breakfast and dinner. It offers basic but perfectly decent accommodation and has obliging staff. A few rooms have shared bathrooms.
Strada Pieţei 5.
Tel: (0268) 411 080.
www.adabelle.ro

EATING OUT

Bistro Millennium ★★

The international food and service both win plaudits here. Given the classy décor and request for diners to dress up, the prices are lower than you might expect.
Strada Negoiu 14.
Tel: (0268) 412 363.
Open: daily noon–midnight.

Bella Muzica ★★★

Serving the unusual combination of Hungarian, Mexican and international dishes, this cosy downstairs eatery, shaped like a tunnel, has circumvented the nuisance of inattentive Romanian waiting staff by giving each table a small button which alerts your waiter to your need. As well as the food menu, you can also choose your own music from a list of CDs.
Strada Gheorghe Bariţiu 2.
Tel: (0268) 477 946.
www.bellamuzica.ro.
Open: daily noon–midnight (last orders 11pm).

Casa Hirscher ★★★

A wide range of Italian favourites is served up in three large rooms, decorated with coats of arms, as well as at outside tables. Service is quick, prices reasonable and the only downside is the sometimes inappropriate choice of music.
Piaţa Sfatului 12–14 (Strada Apollonia Hirscher).
Tel: (0268) 410 533.
www.casahirscher.ro.
Open: daily noon–midnight.

ENTERTAINMENT

Agenţia Teatrală

Tickets for the city's more high-brow events – classical music, theatre and ballet – can be bought from this ticket agency.
Piaţa Teatrului 1.
Tel: (0268) 471 889.
Open: Tue–Fri 10am–5pm, Sat 10am–2pm.
Closed: Sun & Mon.

Gheorghe Dima Philharmonic

The popular and inexpensive classical concerts here tend to sell out quite far in advance. Things slow down somewhat over the summer months.
Strada Hirscher 10.
Tel: (0268) 473 058.
www.sfbv.home.ro

Haçienda

One of Braşov's top nightspots, the Haçienda is also possibly the largest disco in the country, housed as it is in a former factory.
Strada Carpaţilor 17.
Tel: (0268) 413 971.

Opera Braşov

With a 50-year history, the Braşov Opera House stages mostly big-name shows. Summer tends to be a quiet time.
Strada Bisericii Romane 51.
Tel: (0268) 415 990.
www.opera-brasov.ro

Tetrul Sică Alexandrescu

As well as a regular schedule of plays, recitals, concerts and opera, the theatre also plays host to occasional events such as the city's jazz festival. Tickets, which range from 4 to 9 lei, are on sale from the ticket office just inside the entrance.
Strada Teatrului 1.
Tel: (0268) 418 850.
Ticket office open: Tue–Fri 11am–7pm,
Sat & Sun 3–7pm.
Closed: Mon.

Cluj–Napoca

ACCOMMODATION

Fullton ★★

Very tasteful accommodation in 19 stylish rooms, which variously have wrought-iron furniture, canopies and air-conditioning. The Fullton's location on a quiet back street close to the centre is another plus.
Strada Sextil Puşcariu 10. Tel: (0264) 597 898.
www.fullton.ro

Hotel Meteor ★★

Its central location can result in some noise, despite the double glazing, but this new hotel has a gym, friendly staff, and throws in a buffet breakfast in the adjoining restaurant. Rooms, though not spacious, are bright, cheerful and air-conditioned.
Bulevardul Eroilior 29.
Tel: (0264) 591 060 or 0788 396 582. Email:
reception@hotelmeteor.ro.
www.hotelmeteor.ro

EATING OUT

Red House ★★

Cluj's Magyar heritage is celebrated at this highly reputed restaurant, which offers up Hungarian and Transylvanian favourites.
Strada Constantin Brancuşi 114.
Tel: (0264) 441 829.
Open: daily 11am–11pm.

Roata ★★

Traditional without being cheesy or turgid, Roata serves up tasty, meaty Romanian fare without fuss. Folk music adds to the bustling, lively atmosphere, and there's also a small terrace.
Strada Alexandru Ciura 6A. Tel: (0264) 592 022.
Open: Tue–Sat noon–midnight, Sun–Mon 1pm–midnight.

ENTERTAINMENT

Club Roland Garros

The balcony overlooking the river is the big draw of this place, pizza restaurant-cum-café by day and student disco by night.
Strada Horea 2.
Tel: (0264) 434 952.

The Hungarian State Theatre and Opera House

The Hungarian-language

performances are from time to time translated into Romanian or English. Tickets are on sale from the box office inside.
Strada Emil Isac 26–28. Box office tel: (0264) 593 468. Open: 10am–1pm & 4.30–6.30pm. Opera. Tel: (0264) 593 463. Theatre. Tel: (0264) 593 469.

Obsession
The hugely popular Obsession packs them in (often literally) with theme nights and top DJs.
Strada Republicii 109. Tel: (0264) 401 777. www.obsessionclub.ro

Lacul Roşu
ACCOMMODATION
Vila Bradu ★
Unbeatable for proximity to the lake, the black and white Vila Bradu offers ten rooms that can sleep two or three and around thirty cabins that sleep up to four. There's also a pool and terrace. Breakfast costs extra.
Beside the church. Tel: (0266) 380 042.

Miercurea-Ciuc
ACCOMMODATION
Fenyo ★★★
Very pleasant city-centre accommodation with a gym, massage service, internet access and some rooms equipped for guests with disabilities.
Nicolae Bălcescu 11. Tel: (0266) 311 493. www.hunguest-fenyo.ro

EATING OUT
San Gennaro ★★
Italian-owned eatery in the city's pedestrianised area; food and location both win plaudits.
Strada Pet fi Sándor 15. Tel: (0266) 206 500. www.san-gennaro.ro. Open: daily 9am–midnight.

Poiana Braşov
ACCOMMODATION
Hotel Sport ★★★★
Enjoying an enviable location, the Sport is part of a trio with the Poiana and Bradul hotels, all managed by the same company. It is popular with ski groups, and there are also tennis facilities on site.

50m (55yds) from ski lift. Tel: (0268) 407 333.

EATING OUT
Capra Neagră ★★
Right in the centre of town, the Capra Neagră is divided into a smoking area, a not-as-nice non-smoking area and a conservatory. The place is bright enough, and the cuisine is traditional.
Strada Poiana Soarelui. Tel: (0268) 262 191 or 0788 418 177. www.capraneagra.ro. Open: 24 hours.

SPORT AND LEISURE
Club Rossignol
One-stop-shop for skiers, with quality equipment for hire, a lively après-ski bar and even accommodation. Its location, at the foot of the slopes, is superb.
Opposite main lift. Tel: (0268) 262 470 or 0721 200 470.

Sibiu
ACCOMMODATION
Hotel 11 Euro ★★
It's no longer as cheap as the name implies, but Hotel 11 Euro, housed in

a former clothing factory, has budget rooms within easy walking distance of the centre. Breakfast is extra.

Stada Tudor Vladimirescu 2. Tel: (0269) 222 041 or 0724 691 294. www.11euro.ro

Hotel Ramada ★★★★

The modern and stylish Ramada has tastefully designed rooms and a chic non-smoking restaurant. Early guests included Julio Iglesias.

Strada Emil Cioran 2. Tel: (0269) 235 505. www.ramadasibiu.ro

Hotel Silva ★★★★

A little way out of the centre, this place overlooks the park, and has more of the feel of a mountain chalet hotel than city accommodation. The renovated rooms, some of which have balconies, are done out in red and white, and there's a pleasant terrace.

Strada Aleea Mihai Eminescu 1. Tel: (0269) 243 985. www.hotelsilvasibiu.com

EATING OUT

Grand Plaza ★

Traditional no-nonsense eatery offering all the local staples. Close to the station and charging bargain prices, it's constantly busy.

Strada 9 Mai 60. Tel: (0269) 210 427. Open: Mon–Sat 10am– 11pm. Closed: Sun.

Crama Sibiul Vechi ★★

Former wine cellar turned atmospheric traditional restaurant. Punters pack in for the authentic Transylvanian cuisine (served up by waiters in costume), as well as the live music staged most evenings.

Strada A Papiu Ilarian 3. Tel: (0269) 210 461. www.sibiulvechi.ro. Open daily: noon– midnight.

The Gallery ★★★

Lively, four-level restaurant decorated in tasteful brown, with a fish tank near the entrance (in a purely decorative capacity; the inhabitants are not on the menu). The reasonably priced food is mainly Italian. In good weather some tables are

available on the cobbled streets outside.

Strada Nicolae Bălcescu 37. Tel: 0748 224 807. Open: Mon–Sat 9am– midnight, Sun 11am– midnight.

ENTERTAINMENT

Agenţia Teatrală

The city's ticket agency sells tickets for all the major cultural events.

Strada Nicolae Bălcescu 17. Tel: (0269) 217 575. Open: Mon–Fri 10am– 5pm, Sat & Sun 11am–3pm.

Art Café

Gem of a café that attracts the city's highbrow set (artists, students and German-speakers) who come to enjoy the jazz nights and other cultural happenings or simply to chat and relax. This is a good place to meet some open-minded locals.

Strada Filarmonicii 2. Tel: 0722 265 992.

Chill Out

Trendy nightclub with red sofas and a relaxing terrace. The music is predominantly *electronica*, and there are

regular theme nights.
Piaţa Mică 23.
Tel: 0722 246 640.
www.chilloutsibiu.ro
Sibiu Philharmonic
The Sibiu Philharmonic
has been going strong for
over half a century. A
varied programme brings
in largely European
performers for classical
concerts and recitals.
Tickets, which seldom
go above 20 RON, can
be bought on the night or
from the city's ticket
agency (*see previous
listing*). The city's
International Opera
Festival takes place
around the end of
September.
Strada Cetatii 3–5.
Tel: (0269) 210 264.
www.filarmonicasibiu.ro
**Teatrul Naţional
Radu Stanca**
The majority of
productions here are in
Romanian, with German
offerings on a Wednesday
from time to time. Of
more interest to tourists is
the International Theatre
Festival, to which the
theatre plays host in the
spring.
*Bulevardul Corneliu
Coposu 2.*

Tel: (0269) 210 092.
www.sibfest.ro

SPORT AND LEISURE
Explorer Sport
The shop rents out bikes
and ski equipment, and
will also repair your
cycle. An array of other
outdoor equipment, such
as tents, sleeping bags,
hiking boots, snow
spikes and helmets, is
also on sale. There are
two outlets in Sibiu, and
one in Braşov.
*Strada Calea Dumbravii
14. Tel: (0269) 216 641.*
Strada Turnului 13.
Tel: (0269) 214 744.
www.explorersport.ro

Sighişoara
ACCOMMODATION
**Bed and Breakfast
Coula ★**
The plain exterior of this
400-year-old house belies
a pleasant, family-run
facility that makes guests
feel at home and can also
organise excursions and
activities. In winter, just
one room of the total of
six is available.
Strada Tâmplarilor 40.
Tel: (0265) 777 907.
The Legend House ★★
Five homely rooms, each

with a different theme,
make up this central and
cosy hotel, which also
offers a separate cottage
for groups of four.
Strada Bastionului 8.
Tel: 0744 632 775.
www.legenda.ro
Casa Epoca ★★★
Charming and well-
equipped hotel housed
in a medieval building.
The furnishings are
tasteful, and the cosy
yet modern rooms have
a lot of wood. The
Gothic-style bar and
cavernous restaurant
add character.
Strada Tâmplarilor 40.
Tel: (0265) 773 232.
www.casaepoca.ro

EATING OUT
Casa Cu Cerb ★★
A cavernous place,
serving traditional food
with occasional challenges
for the brave such as
tongue. There are also a
few good fish options.
Strada Şcolii 1. Tel:
(0265) 774 625.
www.casacucerb.ro.
Open: daily 9am–10pm
(summer); Tue 1–9pm,
Wed–Fri 11am–9pm,
Sat–Sun 9am–10pm.
Closed: Mon (winter).

Jo Pizzerie ★★

The excellent views of the citadel, particularly from the terrace, are the main reason to eat at Jo's. The pizza is decent, but it can take a while to get served. More highly rated is the ice cream.
Strada Goga 12.
Tel: (0265) 777 970.
Open: Sun–Thur 10am–midnight, Fri–Sat 10am–1am.

Sighisoara Hotel ★★★

This sizeable hotel-restaurant is nicely decorated, has a good terrace and serves some of the best food in the city. The menu is Romanian with some international dishes.
Strada Şcolii 4–6.
Tel: (0265) 771 000.
www.sighisoarahotels.ro.
Open: daily 7.30–10am & noon–11.30pm (last orders).

ENTERTAINMENT
No Limits

Right beneath the clock tower, you could not get much more in the heart of things than here. No Limits can get busy over the weekend, when the fun goes on until 4am.

Strada Turnului 1A.
Tel: (0265) 518 961 or 0722 593 791.

NORTHERN ROMANIA
Săpânţa
ACCOMMODATION
Pensiunea Stan ★

The five rooms in this yellow pension all have a private bathroom, and there is also hot water, a washing machine, telephone and television. Rooms can be a little heavy on the pink and lace, but are pleasant enough. Breakfast is not included in the room rate.
Strada Principala 406.
Tel: (0262) 372 337.

Satu Mare
ACCOMMODATION
Hotel Dacia ★★

The Secessionist building that houses the Hotel Dacia is also one of the town's main landmarks. The rooms are unable to live up to the high aesthetic standard set by the exterior, but are decent enough, and the hotel's location could not be better. The restaurant is suitably grand.
Piaţa Libertăţii 8.
Tel: (0261) 714 276.

Dana and Dana II ★★★

Brand new pair of hotels with clean, bright rooms, internet connection and professional service. Dana, which is 2km (1¼ miles) south of the city, is slightly cheaper than its newer sister hotel, which is right on the main square.
Dana. Drum Carei 128.
Tel: (0261) 768 716.
Dana II. Piaţa Libertăţii 2. Tel: (0261) 806 230.
www.dana-hotel.ro

EATING OUT
Hotel Dacia ★★

The city's flagship hotel is also one of the few places you might want to eat. Tourists are usually more impressed by the opulent dining room than the food, but there is frequent live music to add to the olde-worlde atmosphere and prices are reasonable.
Piaţa Libertăţii 8.
Tel: (0261) 714 276.
Open: 7am–11.15pm.

ENTERTAINMENT
Dinu Lipatti State Philharmonic

This venue participates in festivals and advertises its

weekly programme on its website. The resident orchestra has toured widely across Europe. Concert tickets are available from the Agenţia Teatrală (*Strada Horea 6. Tel: (0261) 712 106. Open: Mon–Fri 10am–4pm*). The entrance to the venue is set back down a passage beside Hotel Dacia.
Piaţa Libertăţii 8. Tel: (0261) 712 666. www.filarmonicasm.ro

Suceava
ACCOMMODATION
High Class Hostel ★★
Free tea and coffee, brand new furniture and very friendly and helpful staff make High Class Hostel, which moved to a new location in late 2007, a favourite among backpackers. Monastery tours can also be arranged.
Strada Mihai Eminescu 19. Tel: 0723 782 328. www.classhostel.ro
Classic Hotel ★★/★★★
Divided into a 2-star and a 3-star section, this relatively new hotel offers clean, modern accommodation with the main difference being the

size of the rooms and presence or absence of air-conditioning. In the town's university district, the hotel is a short walk from the main action.
Strada Universităţii 32 & 36. Tel: (0230) 510 000 or 0741 082 304. www.classic.ro

EATING OUT
Latino ★★★
Held by many to be the town's best restaurant, this Italian is famed for its quality food, unusually professional service and stylish interior. Given its universally agreed excellence, the prices offer great value. Unsurprisingly, it can get busy.
Strada Curtea Domnească 9. Tel: (0230) 523 627. Open: daily 11am–midnight.
Piccolo Mondo ★★★
Housed in a large, pale yellow villa, this should not be confused with the Lebanese restaurant of the same name in Bucharest. This place serves upmarket Romanian food, with an emphasis on game dishes.

Strada Petru Rareş 21. Tel: (0230) 522 837 or 0741 331 990.

ENTERTAINMENT
Club 60
Jazz, blues, rock, soul and hiphop are among the genres on offer here, and live bands sometimes make an appearance. The vibe is relaxed, aided in no small part by the comfortable sofas.
Strada Ştefan cel Mare. Tel: (0230) 209 440.
Office's Club
Based on the interior of an English pub, the trendy Office's Club brings in DJs to entertain the cocktail-sipping clientele. Until 11pm you can also order food.
Strada Corneliu Coposu. Tel: (0230) 209 279. www.officesclub.ro

Vatra Dornei
ACCOMMODATION
Hotel Maestro ★★
Very pretty hotel with eight respectable if smallish rooms and a great terrace at the front. Other facilities include a Jacuzzi and a sauna. The restaurant also enjoys an excellent reputation.

Strada Republicii 1.
Tel: (0230) 375 379.
www.hotelmaestro.ro

EATING OUT
Les Amis ★
The service may be
reluctant and the music
too loud, but for location
Les Amis is hard to beat.
The menu is also
translated into English.
Strada Luceafărului 15.
Tel: (0230) 371 280.
Open: daily 9am–11pm.

Vişeu de Sus
ACCOMMODATION
Hotel Brad ★★
Popular in summer,
this small hotel has
plain but comfortable
rooms – it is worth
calling ahead.
Strada 22 Decembrie 50.
Tel: (0262) 352 999.
Hotel Gabriela ★★
A short walk from the
town itself, this is a
relatively swanky option
with in-room fridges and
mini-bars. The large
restaurant, which serves
traditional Romanian
food, has a terrace.
Strada Randunelelor 1.
Tel: (0262) 354 380 or
0741 370 384.
www.hotel-gabriela.ro

Voroneţ
ACCOMMODATION
Casa Elena ★★★
A 4-star facility, rooms at
Casa Elena, divided into
five separate buildings,
have been done out in
style. The hotel offers
various sports facilities
and internet access.
At the entrance to Voroneţ
village. Tel: (0230) 235
326 or 0744 757 719.

THE BLACK SEA COAST AND DANUBE DELTA
Constanţa
ACCOMMODATION
Hotel Ferdinand ★★★
Central and modern
3-star hotel, with
in-room internet access
and fridges.
Bulevardul Ferdinand
12. Tel: (0341) 407 761.
www.hotelferdinand.ro
Ibis ★★★
The reliable Ibis chain
now has a branch in
Constanţa. The hotel has
a casino, gym, sauna,
Jacuzzi, massage centre,
bowling alley and Wi-fi
internet access.
Strada Mircea cel
Batran 39–41.
Tel: (0241) 508 050.
www.accorhotels.com

EATING OUT
Casa Ana ★★
It seems to have changed
little since Communist
times, but Casa Ana is a
restful, bright and
pleasant place to dine,
with a traditional
Romanian menu and big
portions. It's particularly
popular with tourists.
Bulevardul Tomis 17.
Tel: (0241) 553 999.
Open: daily 10am–10pm.
Marco Polo ★★★
Highly reputed Italian
restaurant decorated with
plants. Pizza, pasta, meat
mains, fish, salads and
desserts are all top notch
and, as a refreshing
change, there is a decent
choice for vegetarians.
Strada Mircea cel Bătrân
103. Tel: (0241) 617 537
or 0722 230 976. Open:
daily 11am–midnight.

ENTERTAINMENT
Cinema Studio
The cinema shows
relatively new foreign-
language releases.
Bulevardul Tomis 38.
Tel: (0241) 611 358.
Teatrul Dramatic
Metamorfoze Constanţa
This theatre also
incorporates the Black

Sea Philharmonic and the Oleg Danovski Ballet Theatre. Tickets can be bought either from the ticket office (*Bulevardul Tomis 97. Open: Mon–Fri 9am–6pm, Sat 9am–noon, Sun 5–6.50pm*) or from the Agenție de Bilete (*Strada Ștefan cel Mare 34. Open: 10am–5pm*). *Strada Mircea cel Bătrân 97. Tel: (0241) 615 268.*

SPORT AND LEISURE
Delphi
Delphi arranges diving courses in the Black Sea.
Bulevardul Mamaia 19. Tel: 0722 336 686. www.divingdelphi.ro

Costinești
ACCOMMODATION
Admiral Nord ★★
A new hotel close to the station, this 2-star option is one of the better places to stay in the resort. Breakfast is not included in the price.
By the station. Tel: (0241) 734 944.

EATING OUT
Albert Pizza ★★
Decorated in bright yellow and green, this huge pizzeria serves a mix of Romanian and Italian food and has a good view of the beach.
North side of the lake. Open: daily 6am–midnight.

Eforie Nord
ACCOMMODATION
Vila Horiana ★★★
Friendly, homely and intimate pension. The four rooms, some of which have a private balcony, sleep up to four each, and a highlight is the tasty home cooking.
Strada Alexandru Cuza 13. Tel: (0241) 741 388.
Europa ★★★★
Widely regarded as one of Romania's best spas, the 4-star Europa also has a swimming pool.
Bulevardul Republicii 13. Tel: (0241) 741 710.

EATING OUT
El Stefanino ★★
Quaint eatery with wrought-iron furniture, canopies, a sea view and helpful staff. The menu is the typical coast menu of Romanian plus pizza.
Bulevardul Tudor Vladimirescu 6. Tel: (0241) 735 484 or 0722 515 704.

Eforie Sud
ACCOMMODATION
Hotel Edmond ★★★
Newly opened 3-star hotel just a minute from the beach, with sauna and Jacuzzi.
Strada Dezrobirii 26. Tel: (0241) 748 522 or 0721 259 230.

EATING OUT
Han Dobrogea ★★
As Romanian-looking as you can get, the large and shady Han Dobrogea has folk costumes, wooden tables and rustic red tablecloths. The menu is Romanian plus pizza.
Bulevardul Republicii 39. Open: daily 8am–midnight.

Jupiter
ACCOMMODATION
Sat Vacanta
Liliacul ★★★
Newly opened 3-star bungalow offering apartment-style accommodation.
Centre of town. Tel: (0241) 731 169.

EATING OUT
Rustika ★★
Open for the summer season, this pleasant and professional place serves the usual seaside combination of traditional Romanian plus pizza. The largely wooden interior also includes trees and a bridge to a different section. Phone ahead to organise discounts for groups. It is particularly popular with Russians.
Centre of town, next to Café Marharitas. Tel: 0722 606 818. Open: daily noon–midnight.

Mamaia
ACCOMMODATION
Hotel Midia ★
Budget Midia has 124 rooms with private bathroom. The rooms are small without TVs but offer good value for money. The cheerful staff is another bonus.
Bulevardul Mamaia. Tel: (0241) 831 940.
Hotel Bulevard ★★★★
Fitness, sauna, massage and complementary therapies are among the options at this modern facility. It's not cheap, but the standards are high.
Bulevardul Mamaia 294. Tel: (0241) 831 533. www.complexbulevard.ro

EATING OUT
La Mama ★★
No-frills Romanian fare that appeals to foreigners wanting to sample the local cuisine in a clean, pleasant venue. There are several outlets in Bucharest, where the chain began.
Faleza Casino. Tel: 0730 526 262. www.lamama.ro
La Fattoria ★★★
Seaside branch of the Bucharest chain of upmarket Italians. The main restaurant is opposite a separate section that does a great range of cakes and light meals. The latter is right by the beach.
Zona Majestic. Tel: (0241) 831 010 or 0729 881 010. www.lafattoria.ro. Open: daily 10.30–1am.

ENTERTAINMENT
Club Gossip
The old Motor Club has been re-launched as Club Gossip. There are themed nights, such as hiphop and R&B, and DJ parties.
Bulevardul Mamaia 218. Tel: 0723 311 556.
Goa Club
Trendy club and lounge that brings in foreign DJs.
Former casino building on Bulevardul Mamaia. Tel: 0730 000 462.

Neptun
ACCOMMODATION
Albert Hotel ★★★
Just 400m (437 yds) from the beach, the Albert is ranked among the top Black Sea hotels. It has 55 well-equipped doubles and 7 apartments, all tastefully decorated.
Between Neptun & Olimp. Tel: (0241) 731 514.

EATING OUT
Mediterraneo ★★★
Friendly staff, appropriate music and a tasteful interior with lots of wood make this large, clean place one of the best places to eat in Neptun. The menu is the usual mix of Romanian and international.

Centre of Neptun. Tel:
(0241) 701 107. Open:
daily 9am–midnight
(Oct–May), non-stop
(June–Sept).

Sfântu Gheorghe
ACCOMMODATION
Pensuine Mareea ★★★
Simple, rustic
accommodation and
excellent home-cooked
meals. The owners can
also help you arrange
trips into the delta.
Near the dock.
Tel: (0240) 531 086 or
0744 306 389.
www.mareea.go.ro

Sulina
ACCOMMODATION
Pensuinea Ana ★
This friendly pension has
four double rooms, a
terrace and a garden.
Strada IV 144.
Tel: (0240) 543 252 or
0724 421 976.
Casa Coral ★★
One of the poshest
places to stay in town,
this 3-star waterfront
hotel has 15 decent
rooms and pleasant
outside areas.
Strada I 195.
Tel: (0240) 543 777 or
0742 974 016.

Tulcea
ACCOMMODATION
Hotel Delta ★★★
Comfortable and well-
equipped hotel housed in
a Communist building.
Following modernisation,
the place now features a
swimming pool and a
fitness centre. The
service is good, and there
is wheelchair access,
although prices are a
little on the high side.
Strada Isaccei 2.
Tel: (0240) 514 270.
www.deltahotelro.com
Rex ★★★★
The 4-star Rex has large,
air-conditioned rooms
and helpful, professional
staff.
Strada Toamnei 1.
Tel: (0240) 511 351.
www.hotelrex.ro

EATING OUT
Restaurant Select ★★★
Widely agreed to be the
city's top restaurant,
Select offers fine dining
in an upmarket and
decorous atmosphere. The
varied menu, presented in
six languages, includes a
lot of fish – as you'd
expect in the delta – as
well as local, national and
international staples.

Strada Păcii 6.
Tel: (0240) 510 301.

ENTERTAINMENT
Danubia
Restaurant, bar and club
in one. The disco, Keops,
is slightly livelier than
King's Club, although
the latter can also get
busy and it can be worth
booking a table in
advance.
Strada Portului 2.
Tel: (0240) 514 732.

Vama Veche
ACCOMMODATION
Lyana ★
This beachfront location
affords great views,
provided you can put up
with the noise. Popular
with the hippie and
alternative crowd, Lyana
also has a restaurant, one
of the resort's few decent
options.
On the beach. Tel: 0744
671 213.

EATING OUT
Bibi Bistro ★★
Relaxed beach-hut-style
place with large tables
and good, typical
Romanian food.
Just off the beach.
Tel: 0722 241 216.

Index

Acknowledgements

Thomas Cook wishes to thank VASILE SZAKACS for the loan of the photographs reproduced in this book, to whom copyright in the photographs belongs, except the following:

DAMIEN BOILLEY (131)

DREAMSTIME CF Dumitrescu (40), C Iacobut (97), B Lazar (22), C Portasa Bogdan (61), T Stanica (41, 46), P Stellan (60)

For CAMBRIDGE PUBLISHING MANAGEMENT LTD:

Project editor: DIANE TEILLOL

Copy editor: ANNE McGREGOR

Typesetter: TREVOR DOUBLE

Proofreader: JOANNE OSBORN

Indexer: MARIE LORIMER

SEND YOUR THOUGHTS TO BOOKS@THOMASCOOK.COM

We're committed to providing the very best up-to-date information in our travel guides and constantly strive to make them as useful as they can be. You can help us to improve future editions by letting us have your feedback. If you've made a wonderful discovery on your travels that we don't already feature, if you'd like to inform us about recent changes to anything that we do include, or if you simply want to let us know your thoughts about this guidebook and how we can make it even better – we'd love to hear from you.

Send us ideas, discoveries and recommendations today and then look out for your valuable input in the next edition of this title.

Emails to the above address, or letters to Travellers Series Editor, Thomas Cook Publishing, PO Box 227, Unit 9, Coningsby Road, Peterborough PE3 8SB, UK.

Please don't forget to let us know which title your feedback refers to!